A PRIMER OF LITERARY CRITICISM

G.E. Hollingworth

ATLANTIC
PUBLISHERS & DISTRIBUTORS (P) LTD

ATLANTIC
PUBLISHERS & DISTRIBUTORS (P) LTD
7/22, Ansari Road, Darya Ganj, New Delhi
Tel.: +91-11-4077 5252, 2327 3880
E-mail: orders@atlanticbooks.com
Web: www.atlanticbooks.com

Published by Atlantic Publishers & Distributors (P) Ltd 2024

Printed & bound in India by Atlantic Print Services

PREFACE

There has been of late years an increasing tendency to require, of those who are studying English Literature, some ability to describe the impression which it makes on them, and to show how the author succeeds in producing that impression.

Some learners may be able to do this spontaneously, but in most cases help in the form of hints and worked examples will be necessary.

This *Primer* — for it is intended to be no more than a primer — is an attempt to supply the necessary help, and is written throughout from the beginner's point of view. For practical purposes it seemed well to deal somewhat more fully with short passages which can be printed in full than with complete works to which general reference only can be made.

It is assumed that the book will be used as a companion to the observant reading of English Classics, not as a substitute for that reading. This has been borne in mind in the numerous exercises which follow each chapter, and which the teacher or even the learner will have no difficulty in fitting by selection and adaptation to the particular works with which he is himself concerned.

In the Index will be found not only references to the body of the work, but also dates and such information with regard to writers mentioned as is required in order that the reader may understand what is said about them.

In dealing with contemporary literature, no attempt has been made to cover the ground at all completely : the authors mentioned have been chosen on the score of their appeal to the beginner or of the distinctive character of their style rather than for their intrinsic literary worth.

G.E. HOLLINGWORTH

CONTENTS

1

What is Style?

1. Style is regarded by some people as useless ornamentation, much liked by schoolmasters but of no value to the ordinary man. Yet style is in reality everybody's concern : it is merely the way in which we write; we all have a style, though some of us have a very bad one. Try to recollect the last "good story" you heard spoilt in the telling, and you will find that its failure to provoke a laugh was wholly due to faults of style — bad arrangement, perhaps, or wordiness or lack of clearness. Style is, however, a great deal more than freedom from obvious faults, such as prolixity and obscurity : a tale told in a clear, straightforward way is not necessarily told well. Take, for instance, the death of Colonel Newcome, one of the most pathetic scenes in literature.

Some time afterwards Ethel came in with a scared face to our pale group. "He is calling for you again, dear lady," she said, going up to Madame de Florac, who was still kneeling; "and just now he said he wanted Pendennis to take care of his boy. He will not know you." She hid her tears as she spoke.

She went into the room where Clive was at the bed's foot; the old man within it talked on rapidly for a while : then again he would sigh and be still : once more I heard him say hurriedly, "Take care of him when I'm in India"; and then with a heart-rending voice he called out, "Léonore, Léonore!" She was kneeling by his side now. The patient's voice sank into faint murmurs; only a moan now and then announced that he was not asleep.

At the usual evening hour the chapel bell began to toll, and Thomas Newcome's hands outside the bed feebly beat time. And just as the last bell struct, a peculiar sweet smile shone over his face, and he lifted up his head a little, and quickly said, "Adsum!" and fell back. I was the word we used at school, when names were called; and lo, he, whose heart was as that of a little child, had answered to his name, and stood in the presence of The Master.

Now let us give the same account in a clear, straightforward way.

"By and by Ethel came in, looking scared like the rest of us. She went up to Madame de Florac, who was still on her knees, and said to her, "He wants you again, and a minute or two ago he said Pendennis was to look after his boy." "He is incapable," she added, as she furtively wiped her eyes, "of recognising you."

2. There is no need to go on : nobody would shed tears over the re-written death-bed scene. Yet it "says the same things." No, that is exactly what it does not do. Thackeray's words are simple words that bring with them memories of everyday life; but they are so selected and arranged that the impression they give is never commonplace, never lacking in dignity : the sentences are very short, so that they seem like echoes of the little, jerky, restrained phrases that we all use when we can scarcely master our grief. The second version has none of these merits; where it uses simple words they are, as our grandmothers would have said, "low." "Looking scared like the rest of us" : there is almost a humorous ring about that; " a minute or two ago" — that is one of the vague and colourless expressions which we have worn out by constant use; "wiped her eyes" — that is too concrete; it calls up a picture of a blubbered face and a pocket-handkerchief. The trailing sentences with their loosely-linked co-ordinate and subordinate clauses are suited not to the expression of restrained grief, but to hurried and rather inconsequential narrative.

Our anonymous bungler, too, appears to think that pathos is helped by words of Latin origin. "Incapable, added, furtively, recognising" — all these he uses where he hopes to affect us most. He is wrong. These are not the simple words which we hear as children from our mothers; they are words which we learn at school, and they bring with them memories of thinking instead of feeling. "Added" suggests sums, "incapable" suggests estimates of ability — school reports, angry masers, testimonials, "drunk and incapable" — "furtively" suggests slyness and cunning, detective tales and theft. If you compare the two versions, you will perhaps find some more faults in the account which aims merely at being "clear and straightforward."

Nor is it only when we wish to be funny or pathetic that we need a good style : style is just as important if an author would terrify, horrify, excite, or merely interest his readers.

3. What then is syle? Style is the body to which thought is the soul, and through which it expresses itself. And, in literature at least,

"Of the soul the body form doth take;
For soul is form, and doth the body make."

It varies from the outworn phrase and faulty syntax of the fifth-rate journalist to the perfection of Francis Thompson's

I shook the pillaring hours
And pulled my life upon me.

4. Those of us who find even the composition of a simple letter a task involving rough drafts, may despair of ever being able to express our deepest feelings; it is not for us, we think, to describe moonlight on wet glades or compose poems in honour of our lady-love.

But our forefathers were not so inarticulate. When the Angles gathered round the fire at night, each was expected to sing a poem. Cædmon, the stableman, who knew no songs, slunk away in shame. Of course, not every farm-labourer composed immortal verse — only the great bards could do that — but even farm-labourers were expected to remember long poems, most could fill up with original matter any gaps in their memory, and many could turn a tale or a sentiment into artistic form. Probably printing and the spread of education have made us lose the faculty. We read more and speak less; knowledge is no longer handed down by oral tradition; we have grown less sensitive to the *sound* of words, more at home with purely intellectual concepts.

5. Yet we are all, or nearly all, born with the story-telling and word-tasting faculties; quite young children will invent tales and jingle rimes and decide that a new word is "funny" or "ugly" or "pretty." There is no need for the dullest of us to despair. We cannot all be Shakespeares; but we can all, with a little patience, learn to understand and love great prose and verse, learn to choose and arrange our words with an artist's care.

EXERCISE I

1. Here are some more passages from great authors accompanied by versions written by an anonymous bungler. Decide in each case which is the original version, and write down a list of the points in which it is superior to the copy. Make your list as complete as possible.

(i) (*a*) Nothing in history or fiction, not even the story which Ugolino told in the sea of everlasting ice, after he had wiped his bloody lips on the scalp of his murderer, approaches the horrors which were recounted by the few survivors of that night. They cried for mercy. They strove to burst the door. Holwell who, even in that extremity, retained some presence of mind, offered large bribes to the gaolers. But the answer was that nothing could be done without the Nobob's orders, that the Nabob was asleep, and that he would be angry if anyone woke him. Then the prisoners went mad with despair. They trampled each other down, fought for the places at the windows, fought for the pittance of water with which the cruel mercy of the murderers mocked their agonies, raved, prayed, blasphemed, implored the guards to fire among them. The gaolers in the mean time held lights to the bars, and shouted with laughter at the frantic struggles of their victims.

At length the tumult died away in low gaspings and moanings. The day broke. The Nabob had slept off his debauch, and permitted the door to be opened. But it was some time before the soldiers could make a lane for the survivors, by piling up on each side the heaps of corpses on which the burning climate had already begun to do its loathsome work. When at length a passage was made, twenty-three ghastly figures, such as their own mothers would not have known, staggered one by one out of the charnel-house. A pit was instantly dug. The dead bodies, a hundred and twenty-three in number, were flung into it promiscuously, and covered up.

(*b*) That night was very horrible. The victims, after in vain begging for mercy, trying to break out, and offering bribes to their gaolers, became panic-stricken. At length their struggles for water and air ceased; and, when the Nabob next morning allowed the door to be opened, the survivors, twenty-three in number, came out. The dead, who numbered a hundred and twenty-three, were buried in one grave. The survivors were terribly changed.

(ii) (*a*) Now will I go to Innisfree,
And will build a rustic shed in a glade,
With bean rows and a hive for the bee.
I will live alone in the hut I have made.

(*b*) I will arise and go now, and go to Innisfree,
And a small cabin build there, of clay and wattles made;
Nine bean rows will I have there, a hive for the honey-bee,
And live alone in the bee-loud glade.

(iii) (*a*) She looked up. Heaven was almost emptied of stars. Such as still lingered shone with a changed and waning brightness, and began to faint in their stations. And the colour of the sky itself was the most wonderful; for the rich blue of the night had now melted and softened and brightened; and there had succeeded in its place a hue that has no name, and that is never seen but as the herald of morning. "O!" she cried, joy catching at her voice, "O! it is the dawn!"

(*b*) When she looked up, she saw that most of the stars were set, and the rest were growing faint. The colour of the sky was extremely beautiful — a softer and brighter blue than that of the night, a colour which one only sees just before dawn. "O!" she said, in a voice broken with happiness, "the morning is coming."

(iv) (*a*) Dark to me is the earth. Dark to me are the heavens.
Where is she that I loved, the woman with eyes like stars?
Desolate are the streets. Desolate is the city.
A city taken by storm, where none are left but the slain.

(*b*) Sky and earth are dark to me,
Drear and dread the city lies.
Where is she gone, who had star-like eyes?
The streets seem dark when I cannot see
Her whom I loved; and the city lies spread
Like a captured city filled with dead.

2. Nancy is a poor girl, brought up as a member of a vile gang. She comes to desire a better life, and meets in secret a lady who is interested in her. Bill Sikes, a brutal member of the gang, whom she loves, convinced that she is betraying them, bursts into her room and murders her. Write the murder scene. When you have written it, turn to *Oliver Twist*, Chapter 47, and see where and why Dicken's account is more thrilling than yours.

3. Years ago Peter Jenkyns, when a lad, bored by life in a small town, dressed himself up as his elder and very staid sister, and walked about with an imitation baby in his arms. A crowd collected, Peter's father came up, saw what had happened, snatched the pillow from Peter, and thrashed the lad. Tell the tale in the person of Miss Matty, his other sister, who is now an old woman. Compare your account with Mrs. Gaskell's *Cranford*, Chapter 6.

4. Compare with the account of the death of Colonel Newcome as many as you can of the following death scenes : —

Little Nell (*Old Curiosity Shop*, Chapter 62), Jo (*Bleak House*, Chapter 47), Mr. Dorrit (*Little Dorrit*, Chapter 19), Dora (*David Copperfield*, Chapter 53), Sidney Carton (*Tale of Two Cities*, Chapter 35), Maggie Tulliver (*Mill on the Floss*, last chapter), Falstaff (*Henry* V., II. iii.), Lear (*Lear*, V. iii.), Smike (*Nicholas Nickleby*, Chapter 58), Sir Roger de Coverley (*Spectator*, No. 517), Amy Robsart (*Kenilworth*, Chapter 41), Tess (*Tess of the D'Urbervilles*, Chapter 59), Front de Bœuf (*Ivanhoe*, Chapter 31), Bill Sikes (*Oliver Twist*, Chapter 50), Barkis (*David Copperfield*, Chapter 30). Which of these do you think the most pathetic? Which the most horrible? or exciting? or grotesque? or tragic? Try to account for the effect they have upon you. Do any of them seem to you faulty? In what way?

5. A boy of eight, who has been spoilt by his widowed mother, is dying from consumption. Write a death-bed scene.

6. Read the account of the burning of Torquilstone (*Ivanhoe*, Chapter 32). Write a description of a fire in a slum.

7. Read the description of the flood in *The Mill on the Floss* (last chapter). Imagine that your riverside bungalow is flooded; write a letter to a friend, telling him your adventures.

8. Read the storm scene in *David Copperfield* (Chapter 55). Imagine that Steerforth was saved by Ham, and is telling David what he felt. Give his account.

2

The Elements of Style

6. You have now, especially if you have worked through Exercise I, seen that a good style is an essential part even of a good story. We have next to consider what it is that makes style.

7. First of all, a good style is one that is suitable for its purpose — you would not write a funeral sermon in the style of Mark Twain, or a chemical treatise in triolets. But that does not take us very far. Shelley's or Chesterton's style is suitable for its purpose : why and how is it suitable? Why is it that *Paradise Lost* written by Chesterton would be something entirely different from the epic we have? Because Chesterton and Milton have, in the first place, a different set of ideas and a different outlook; and, in the second, a different way of expressing their ideas. This, then, gives us our two main elements of style — choice of ideas and expression of ideas, though in the best styles the two are inseparably interwoven.

A. CHOICE OF IDEAS

8. At the bottom of the scale comes the writer whose sole aim is to impart information. For him there is scarcely any choice : the facts are there, and he has merely to state them. But as soon as he wishes to interest or amuse, persuade or sadden, a writer has to select his facts.

General or Particular; Abstract or Concrete

9. He may merely state general principles; he may illustrate general principles by particular cases. Note the use of detail on

p. 4; it is one of the things which distinguish Macaulay from Mr. Dry-as-Dust. Not that detail is always desirable; Macaulay himself points out that Milton, instead of giving exact details, uses "dim intimations," so that Heaven and Hell, angels and devils are for us remote and sublime, shrouded in mystery.

But if the general and the abstract wisely used give a greater spaciousness, a sense of the sublime and the awe-inspiring, the detailed and the concrete make a more vivid impression.

> He, above the rest
> In shape and gesture proudly eminent,
> Stood like a tower. His form had yet not lost
> All her original brightness, nor appeared
> Less than Archangel ruined, and the excess
> Of glory obscured.

That does not give us a clear picture of Satan; but we can *see* Keats's Autum —

> Sometimes whoever seeks abroad may find
> Thee sitting careless on a granary floor,
> Thy hair soft-lifted by the winnowing wind;
> Or on a half-reap'd furrow sound asleep,
> Drowsed with the fume of poppies.

Visualisation

10. Nor is it only the greater amount of detail which makes the picture real. Keats has the power of visualisation; he makes us see Autumn because he himself sees her more clearly than if she were actually a living person before him. He does not say, " Let me personify the idea of Autumn and give her appropriate attributes." Gray too often does —

> And Truth severe, by fairer Fiction dress'd.

This power of visualisation varies immensely in individuals; some of us have a bright mental image of our uncle or the cook as soon as we hear their names, others can with difficulty recall whether their noscs turn up or clown. But none of us can hope to equal Chaucer and Dickens, whose slightest sketches have a startling aliveness.

Not all detail, however, is explanatory, interest-giving detail as in a guide-book, or beautiful or grotesque picture-detail like Tennyson's or Lewis Carroll's. Carlyle is fond of detail which suggests motion — "stands or sprawls up;" Pope's mind no sooner calls up one idea than it finds another to compare or contrast with it — "a timorous foe, and a suspicious friend;" the emotions and thoughts of Meredith's and Browning's characters are treated exhaustively, but we have no clear picture of Sludge the Medium or Diana of the Crossways in the flesh.

Kind of Idea

11. The kind of idea used, indeed, is an excellent, index to the author's mind and tastes : to Swift most things suggest the disgusting; we can trace the architect in Hardy, the artist-decorator in Morris. The writer of uncertain taste will use inappropriate ideas — mixing the sad with the merry or the commonplace with the sublime, like Donne often and Milton sometimes; Ella Wheeler Wilcox is commonplace, Bacon pregnant, Browne subtle and exalted.

B. EXPRESSION OF IDEAS

The charm of all writing is a nice mingling of the familiar and the unfamiliar. Like the Athenians, we seek always some new thing; but the entirely now, if it existed, would be too great a strain upon our imagination and credulity. Good style is in the main a matter of the perfect use of contrast and similarity, the new and the old.

Repetition

12. In the sphere of expression, repetition — either of idea or of phrase — is perhaps the simplest, as it is one of the oldest, ways of linking new and old. Folk-tales and ballads are full of it, from Cinderella's three nights at the ball and the tale of *The Three Little Pigs* who built houses, to *Edom O'Gordon* and *Binnorie.* The parallelism of the *Psalms* —

> Keep thy tongue from evil, and thy lips from speaking guile.

Depart from evil and do good;
Seek peace, and pursue it.

the refrain of the mediaeval lyric—

Timor Mortis conturbat me,

or the modern music-hall song are examples of the same tendency. But the great poets can get from it an exquisite music and a wonderful suggestiveness. Take Tennyson's *Break, break, break.*

Break, break, break,
On thy cold gray stones, O Sea!
And I would that my tongue could utter
The thoughts that arise in me.

O well for the fisherman's boy,
That he shouts with his sister at play
O well for the sailor lad
That he sings in his boat on the bay

And the stately ships go on
To their haven under the hill;
But O for the touch of a vanish'd hand,
And the sound of a voice that is still!

Break, break, break,
At the foot of thy crags, O Sea!
But the tender grace of a day that is dead
Will never come back to me.

Here the threefold *Break* of the first line is caught up at the end, to be followed each time by a similar but different phrase. In the second stanza again, the first two lines are exactly parallel in structure to the second two, while the repeated *O* forms a slight link between the second and third stanzas. In the third stanza the last two lines are again similar in construction. The suggestion — for it is no more — of a refrain obtained in this way fills the poem with a wistful and haunting melody, and at the same time recalls the slow inwash and shattering of the waves, continuous but irregular.

Tennyson's *Crossing the Bar* gets, in the same way, something of the same effect; *Go not, happy day*, in his *Maud* uses repetition in a dainty pirouette of delight; in *The Passing of Arthur* the three journeys of Sir Bedivere, himself so often "bold," to the lake, gives another perfect example of repetition modified so that the phrases are at once old and new; Swinburne's long soliloquy of Iseult at Tintagel is set in a wonderful framework of storm, and is broken at intervals by semi-repetitions —

> And swordlike was the sound of the iron wind,
> And as a breaking battle was the sea.
>
> . . . . . .
>
> And as a full field charging was the sea,
> And as the cry of slain men was the wind.
>
> . . . . . .
>
> And all her soul was as the breaking sea,
> And all her heart anhungered as the wind.

which reflect and emphasise Iseult's wild prayer at the same time as they break it up into sections and so prevent monotony.

This apparently simple method, indeed, is capable of infinite modulations, each giving a different effect. Compare, for their varying shades of anguish, the cry of David,

> O my son, Absalom! O Absalom, my son, my son!

of Samson Agonistes, lamenting his blindness,

> O dark, dark, dark, amid the blaze of noon,
> Irrecoverably dark, total eclipse
> Without all hope of day!

and of Lear to his unnatural daughters,

> You think I'll weep;
> No, I'll not weep :
> I have full cause of weeping; but this heart
> Shall break into a hundred thousand flaws,
> Or ere I'll weep.

or, most poignant of all, Lear's cry as he bends over the dead Cordelia,

No, no, no life!
Why should a dog, a horse, a rat, have life,
And thou no breath at all? Thou'lt come no more,
Never, never, never, never, never!

The fortieth chapter of Isaiah uses the Same means for the exquisite restfulness of verses 1 and 2, the despairing cry of verses 6-8, and the ecstatic joy of verse 9. Note, too, the cumulative menace in Isaiah, chapters ix. and x. of the refrain, "For all this His anger is not turned away, but His hand is stretched out still"; and the lyrical delight expressed by the similarities of construction in I. Corinthians, xiii.

Yet, at the other end of the scale, we have comic repetition, conscious —

O Sally Brown, O Sally Brown!
How could you serve me so?

or unconscious —

O Sophonisba, Sophonisba, O!

Then, again, there are Dickens's repeated references to characteristics or mannerisms of his personages — Mrs. Gamp's constant allusions to Mrs. 'Arris, Mrs. Micawber's "I will never desert Mr. Micawber," Mr. Cruncher's spiky hair, and Mrs. Cruncher's "flopping." Or you may have the repetition of situation as in *Geraint and Enid;* the symmetrical love affairs of *A Midsummer Night's Dream;* the exactly similar hoaxing of Beatrice and Benedick in *Much Ado about Nothing;* the "he childed as I fathered" of *King Lear.*

Perhaps you think you have discovered the secret — repetition means emphasis; emphasise a tragic phrase or situation and you get a tragic effect; emphasise a comic phrase or situation and you get a comic effect. But that is the least part of the secret; the choice of the word, balance and contrast and rhythm — all these are at least as important as the mere repetition. Continue Lear's *Nevers* through another two lines and you have absurdity.

Alliteration

13. The need for moderation is even more evident in another form of repetition — alliteration. Alliteration comes naturally to the English tongue; to our Anglo-Saxon forefathers it was a part of the very structure of verse; and whenever our poetry has been most national — with Langland, the Elizabethans, the Victorians — alliteration has been prominent. Only in the Augustan Age, when we aped France, has it been largely avoided and despised. Yet few things can so soon suggest, artifice instead of art. Shelley's

> Swiftly walk over the western wave,
> Spirit of Night.

is beautiful; so is Swinburne's

> Dreams and desires and sombre songs and sweet;

but, for all its beauty, there is a touch of the mechanical in his

> Before the beginning of years
> There came to the making of man
> Time, with a gift of tears;
> Grief, with a glass that ran.

and the elaborate cross-alliteration of Lyly — *the faith of men, though it fry in their words, it freezeth in their works* — grows intolerably wearisome.

Assonance

14. Assonance, *i.e.* a similarity of vowel sound, is a form of repetition less noticeable to the English ear; a poem which substitutes it for rime misses its mark. But assonance is a great instrument for the playing of word music, as in Spenser's—

> And let the roaring organs loudly play.

Onomatopoeia

15. This line shows too, how assonance may be — and often is — onomatopoeic, that is, may aim at suggesting ideas by imitative sound. Tennysons' lyrics in *The Brook* are an excellent example of this : others are :

The sky-born brook
Chuckled.
The plowman homeward plods his weary way.

You will easily find more in your own reading.

Word-Melody

16. Onomatopoeia and assonance, however, are but part of the choice of melodious words — a choice which again is largely decided by the claims of similarity and contrast. Stevenson has very skilfully shown how much the description of Cleopatra's barge *(Antony and Cleopatra* II., ii. 195-202) depends for its beauty upon the exquisite way in which vowels and consonants are repeated and varied. This is one of those things which distinguish the great poet or prose writer from the little man, though even the greatest may sometimes fail. Shakespeare's —

When first your eye I eyed

is ugly; so is, to come nearer our own day, Hardy's "Death's deaf thrall" : in each case there is too much repetition of sound. In Byron, on the other hand, there is often too much variety : —

Childe Harold had a mother — not forgot
Though parting from that mother he did shun.

is as unmusical as may be. Contrast Shelley's —

Make me thy lyre, even as the forest is :
What if my leaves are falling like its own?
The tumult of thy mighty harmonies
Will take from both a deep autumnal tone.

Read that — as you should read all poetry — aloud, and note its "mighty harmonies." Then analyse the sounds. You will see that the dominant sound is *m;* but it is woven into an intricate pattern of music. First we pass from *m* to *l (lyre, leaves, falling, like)* and *f (forest, falling,* and the related *v* in *even, leaves).* In the next two lines *t* takes its turn *(tumult, mighty, take, autumnal* and *tone).* But there is no sudden break. Our ear has been prepared for it by *forest, what, its :* the *l* sound is not completely, dropped *(tumult, autumnal)* ; even the *f, v* sound *(from)* passes over into the related *th (the, thy, both),* and the *n* sound *(harmonies, autumnal, tone),* itself related to the dominant *m*, echoes *own.* Of the few remaining consonants *k,* the only rugged sound, is harmonised in one case by its use with the liquid *l* and in the other by identity of vowel sound *(make, take);* while the sibilants, always difficult sounds to manage, though beautiful when rightly used, are confined almost entirely to the first two lines *(as, forest, is, leaves, its),* where they admirably suggest the rustle of dead leaves. There is not a jarring note anywhere, and you will find the vowels as skilfully varied as the consonants.

Not, of course, that Shelley planned out his melodies with the scientific exactness of a Bach; be wrote down the words "as they came," merely altering, perhaps, a phrase or two which did not "sound right." Whatever the more sophisticated poet of to-day may do, the older masters wrote by ear, not by rule; and if you think that such an analysis as we have just attempted makes "poetry a mere mechanic art," well, try your own hand at making melodies.

Besides the choice of words, rhythm and sometimes rime help to make word-music. Both of these, again, are based on the same principle of similarity and contrast.

Rime

17. Rime may seem too simple a matter for comment : you may think that a rime is either good or bad, and there is an end of it. It is not even the beginning, for a skilful poet may sometimes deliberately use a false rime as a sort of discord by suspension to be resolved into the harmony of the following perfect rimes. Moreover, there is the comic rime, which gets its effect by surprise, by showing us a similarity we never expected : Butler, Byron, and Browning all loved this :

And though 'tis true that man can only die once,
'Tis not so pleasant in the Gulf of Lyons.

You hope, because you're old and obese,
To find in the furry civic robe ease?

Double or treble rimes, too, even when not in themselves comic, generally sound comic to the Englishman —

Turns out to be a butcher in great business,
Afflicting young folks with a sort of dizziness.

Again, stanza-forms where the rimes come often have usually a more "singing" quality.

You're the maiden posies,
  And so graced
  To be placed
'Fore damask roses.

If the lines are short and the rimes in couplets, there is a danger of doggerel, *e.g.* Butler's *Hudibras* — "scorn made metrical;" if the lines are longer and end-stopped, the couplet rime grows monotonous, though in Pope's verse at its best the sharp snip-snap of the rime emphasises the wit.

On the other hand, the beauty of the sonnet and the Spenserian stanza are due very largely to the satisfaction which the rime gives — a final concord, a resolution of difference into likeness.

Yet, exquisitely melodious as rime can be, many poets have felt that for the sublimest effects it is unsuitable; that it introduces a tinge of prettiness. So anxious are they to avoid a jingle that, in many Ode-forms, the rimes come infrequently enough for the careless reader to overlook them.

Tragedy and epic — the most solemn forms of verse — are almost invariably unrimed. Here the poet depends on that other form of recurrence, rhythm.

Rhythm

18. All rhythm is based on likeness and unlikeness : in prose rhythm, unlikeness predominates; in verse rhythm, likeness. That is to say, poetry has a normal line which sets the measure; the music comes from the variations in the measure. So we get the regular blank verse line : —

And this our life exempt from public haunt.

But a whole speech in this mould would be monotonous; so Shakespeare gives us a speech (*As You Like It*, II. i.) where the pause is varied — now towards the beginning, now in the middle, and now near or at the end of the line; where the stress is varied, trochees being substituted for iambs[1]; where there are extra syllables in the line.

This management of rhythm is an important part of the poet's art; by his rhythm he can express eagerness or weariness, speed or rest, love or hate. Anapaests and-dactyls give swiftness, spondees slowness and dignity, iambs regularity, trochees a ripping movement. Compare the tramp of the horses' feet in Tennyson's *The Charge of the Light Brigade*, the sleepy wistfulness of his *Lotos-Eaters*, the tumultuous passion of his *Locksley Hall*, the sick despair of *Mariana*, the solemn grandeur of his *Passing of Arthur*, and you will see a little — but only a little — of the infinite variety to be obtained.

Prose rhythm is not so easily distinguished, and is for this reason too often ignored. Yet even in "plain" prose it is important — a halting style, with jerky disconnected sentences or long, shapeless, dependent clauses, will ruin the most learned book. In any prose whose first aim is not to impart knowledge but to persuade or to give pleasure, good rhythm is as indispensable as in verse. Read in the Authorised Version Ch. 13 of *1 Corinthians*, and then turn to the Revised Version : the magic is gone. Why? *Love*, to the modern, is at least as beautiful a word as *charity*. But *love* is a single syllable; *charity is* a dactyl; and the whole chapter is set to a rhythm which plays upon dactyl and trochee

---

1. The student with a treacherous memory may like to use Coleridge's lines as a mnemonic :

    Tróchee | tŕips from | lóng to | short.
    From long to long in solemn sort
    Slów Spónd | eé stálks, | stróng fóot | yét ill | able
    Hárdly to | cóme up with | Dáctyl tri | sýllable;
    Iámb | ics márch | from shórt | to lóng;
    With a léap | and a bóund | the swfit Án | apaests thŕong.

Here, as often in speaking of English verse, "long" is used for "stressed syllable," and "short" for "unstressed syllable."

and spondee in such a way that the prevailing effect is dactylic. The substitution of *love* for *charity* destroys the rhythmic scheme : half the emotional appeal is lost.

In your reading, then, do all you can to cultivate your sense of rhythm — it is a sense very highly developed in the young, too often stifled in the adult.

Figures of Speech

19. Rhythm is not the last of the elements of style based on similarity and dissimilarity; there are the figures of speech — smile, metaphor, metonymy, personification, and the pun; antithesis, climax, and anti-climax. Of these the first five are clearly dependent upon comparison, and the next on contrast. Climax and anti-climax are not so evidently developments of the same principle; yet, wben you come to examine them, you will find that climax is nothing but the repetition of an effect with increasing force; while anti-climax, a sudden and unexpected drop in force, gains all its power from the contrast between what we anticipate and what we find.

Do not, then, make the mistake of regarding these figures as arbitrary ornaments of speech : in their origin they are nothing of the kind; they are merely one more expression of that natural impulse of the mind to compare and contrast, to seek similarity and dissimilarity, which we have been considering.

Simile

20. One of the most generally used figures of speech is simile. In common speech we often use it merely as a sort of superlative — "He went like the wind," *i.e.* as quickly as possible, using as an illustration what before the advent of aeroplanes was one of the swiftest things we knew.

21. But if we are imaginative, we shall use simile for many more purposes — to explain, to add vividness, perhaps to provoke a laugh. A child, having seen snow for the first time, may explain that he saw "something called snow, like little bits of ice-cream falling out of the sky — not raspberry ice, but the white kind." This is at once more vivid and more exact than a description of the snow's qualities. So when Henry James says, "Her mind . . . bleated and strayed like an unbranded sheep," we understand immediately what he means. He might have said, "Her mind was unable to think in a logical fashion, could not follow a connected argument, lacked independence, and was not fully under her control;" but that would have been less concise and much duller. Instead he gives us in "bleated" the sense of stupidity and helplessness, in "strayed" the sense of irrelevance and inability to reason, in "unbranded" the sense of something lost and ownerless, in "sheep" the sense of feeble muddle-headedness. In addition, the phrase as a whole suggests the humorous side of her misfortune, partly because the picture it evokes is itself funny, partly because the comparison is unexpected — there is something incongruous between mind, the noblest part of man, and a bleating sheep.

Dickens is, perhaps, our greatest master of the bizarre comparison; you will find it interesting to hunt examples in his novels. Kipling and Chesterton, too, will give you good sport.

22. Just as a simile can add humour, so it can add pathos or awe, terror, or anger.

> Music that gentlier on the spirit lies
> Than tir'd eyelids upon tir'd eyes.
>
> She looks like sleep.
>
> Her tears fall still as oak-leaves after frost.

Each of these is beautiful in a different way. As we read the first, we think of the exquisite softness of deep sleep, the gentle passing from weariness into peace; we catch an atmosphere. The second gives us, as nothing else could, the mingled grace and queenliness of the dead Cleopatra; we see a picture. In the third, too, we see a picture, but here the picture is that of the falling leaves, not that of the weeping woman — the simile has become a little cameo set in the poem; it has an independent existence.

Greek and Latin epic poets were very fond of similes which were even more independent than this, and some of our poets —

notably Spenser, Milton, and Mathew Arnold — have imitated them. For instance, Arnold compares an armed man guarding a bridge to a waggon wedged in the snow blocking a mountain pass. But he is not content with this; his simile — eight lines of blank verse — describes in detail the hinds struggling to urge their cattle round the waggon, the scattering of the snow as they pass, the hot steam rising from the beasts. Before the simile is ended, we have completely forgotten the warder on the bridge.

In this case, then, we must retract our assertion that figures of speech are not ornaments added arbitrarily : in English, at any rate, the "classic simile," beautiful as it is, has an artificial ring. We cannot persuade ourselves that the poet wandered from his subject unintentionally, led astray unconsciously by the picture that the comparison evoked : he has clearly shunted his train deliberately.

Metaphor

23. Metaphor takes the comparison a step further than simile : it identifies the two sides of the comparison. This does not, however, make it more artificial; the poet's mind *sees* the two things as one. Just so the child, if it bad not been told that what it saw was snow, would have said, "It has been raining ice-cream." So we find far more metaphor than simile in Anglo-Saxon poetry; the analysing tendency which turns the feeling of alikeness into a finished comparison comes later. And metaphor has over simile the advantage of brevity; this is why many of the magic phrases of literature are metaphors :

> Man...walketh in a vain shadow.

Here the metaphor says infinitely more than any such bald statement as "Man is deluded." First of all it gives us a picture — a vision of a way-worn and bewildered man stumbling through the mist, as Christian went through the Valley of the Shadow of Death while around him the shapes of Satyrs and Demons gibbered in the darkness. Let us then repeat the words to ourselves and write down a list of the ideas they call up.

"Walketh" suggests action, a mechanical advance, the pilgrimage of life, continuity, monotony, wandering, the weariness of a long journey. "In a vain shadow" suggests emptiness, futility, unreality, mystery, confusion, delusion, blindness, darkness and fear, uncertainty of goal and pathway, the presence behind the unreal shadow of some reality which casts the shadow. These thoughts are what occur to me : you may find others in your lists. We cannot say that the writer intended to convey all these ideas; but they are all there : the beauty and inspiration of literature are as often unconscious as conscious.

24. Consider, again, the line —

How sweet the moonlight sleeps upon this bank.

Try to say that in unfigurative, matter-of-fact language and you cannot : it is like trying to filter bubbles. But one thing is evident : for the poet, the moonlight is a living thing.

25. If he lets this sense of its aliveness grow upon him, he passes easily to personification —

Death lays his icy hand on kings.

Personification

Here again, the poet, the eternal child, is doing what all children do. An imaginative child will talk to its teddy-bear or even to its table and chair and be perfectly convinced that they hear and answer. So, in Keats' *Ode to Autumn*, Autumn is a real person; so, in Shelley's *Cloud*, cloud and sea and sky and sun are living creatures with hopes and fears, joys and sorrows — even, sometimes, a love of practical jokes. This is the true personification.

But there is another kind, beloved of eighteenth century poets, which consists chiefly in the use of capital letters :

Let not Ambition mock their useful toil.

If Memory o'er their tomb no trophies raise.

Can Honour's voice provoke the silent dust,
Or Flatt'ry soothe the dull cold ear of death?

Ambition, Memory, Honour, and Flattery are not alive; we find it impossible to conceive of them as persons performing the actions with which they are credited. The poet is using a mere trick, an ornament, instead of writing what his imagination dictates. His cold intellectualism fails to move us; it is poles asunder from such sincere little cameos as we find in *Lamentations* I. 1-2.

Pathetic Fallacy

26. The same feeling which gives us metaphor and personification is responsible for what Ruskin called the "pathetic fallacy" — the assumption that Nature sympathises with us, the skies weeping when we weep and the sun smiling when we smile. If you would see what a great poet can make of this idea, read the storm scene in *King Lear*; if you would see how the reverse of the idea can intensify grief, read Burns's *Ye Banks and Braes* — here the contrast between happy Nature and human despair adds a poignant irony.

Contrast

27. Indeed contrast is at the base of all irony. What adds the worst sting to sorrow is the remembrance of happiness —

> A sorrow's crown of sorrow is remembering happier things.

We get it over and over again in Hardy's works, this sense of the incongruity between what is and what has been or between what is and what might be. Thus in *My Cicely* the poet, returning after many years, sees — as he thinks — a tombstone to Cicely's memory; and mourns her — dead in her youth. Passing on, he discovers that the Cicely in the churchyard is not the girl he had known; his early love had become the coarse and bibulous ale-wife from whom he had shrunk in disgust, all unconscious of her identity, when first he arrived in the village.

So, too, in *In Memoriam,* Tennyson writes :

> O father, whereso'er thou be
> Who pledgest now thy gallant son;

A shot, ere half thy draught be done,
Hath still'd the life that beat from thee.

O mother, praying God will save
Thy sailor, — while thy head is bow'd,
His heavy-shotted hammock-shroud
Drops in his vast and wandering grave.

A similar irony of situation is found in *Kenilworth* in the manner of Amy Robsart's death.

Incongruity Pun

28. Not, of course, that all contrast is ironic. Often it is humorous. The bizarre comparison has already been considered, the pun —

Said she : My taste will never learn
  To like so huge a man,
So I must beg you will come here
  As little as you can,

makes us smile or groan by the contrast between the two meanings of the word *little*.

But besides these, there are all the other forms of incongruity — the harnessing of unlike ideas —

Smelling of musk and of insolence.

a conjunction which may become still more forcible if coupled with anticlimax —

There thou great Anna, whom three realms obey,
Dost sometimes counsel take and sometimes tea.

the invention of strange beasts — the Cheshire Cat or the Dong with the Luminous Nose; the use of incongruity between an action and the words used to describe it, as in mock-heroic; of incongruity between an action and the performer of it, as when Falstaff pretends to be Henry IV.; of incongruity between persons, as when the mountainous Falstaff is followed by the diminutive page.

You will, indeed, find that homour is generally based on a sense of incongruity — Sam Weller's sayings; Mrs. Jellyby's missionary activities; the temperance zeal of Mr. Stiggins; the alternate despair and hope of Mr. Micawber; the mingled learning and simplicity of Parson Adams, of the Vicar of Wakefield, of Dominie Sampson.

29. Simple contrast is used, too, for relief and to throw into greater prominence; so we get the comic relief of the Porter in *Macbeth,* the grave-diggers in *Hamlet,* the Fool in *King Lear.* Or we have companion pictures, as in Chapter 33 of *Dombey and Son;* contrast in ideas as in Tennyson's *The Two Voices*; contrast in situation as in *The Lady of Shalott,* where there is at first on one side the bustle and life of the world, on the other the unchanging quiet of the Lady; contrast in movement, as when, in the same poem, the sunny, easy lilt which describes the passing of Lancelot changes suddenly to the tragic staccato speed of :

> She left the web, she left the loom;

contrast in character, as in the scene where Lear gives away his kingdom.

Antithesis

30. Antithesis, perhaps the most direct form of contrast, has an appeal more purely intellectual than most figures of speech. You will generally find it in witty prose and verse :

> Damn with faint praise, assent with civil leer,
> And, without sneering, teach the rest to sneer.

Bacon, Dryden, Pope, Johnson, Macaulay, Chesterton — these will afford the best examples. Always antithesis depends for its effect not only upon contrast, but upon balance; the two scales must be evenly weighted.

Climax and Anticlimax

31. In climax and anticlimax, on the other hand, the appeal is due to uneven weighting — one scale is in the air and the other on the ground. Or, to change the comparison, climax starts *pianissimo* and ends *fortissimo;* anticlimax starts *fortissimo* and ends *pianissimo.* Often the two are combined, so that we get first an organ *crescendo,* and then a gradual sinking into silence. Excellent examples are the description of the storm in Tennyson's *Revenge,* the swell and ebb in the description of *The Charge of the Light Brigade,* and Prospero's speech in *The Tempest* about "the cloud-capp'd towers."

32. The figures of speech we have just considered do not, of course, complete the list. The others-metonymy, synecdoche, etc. — are less important, and are often little more than varieties of those we have studied. But there remain a few other elements of style which should not be neglected.

Proper Nouns

33. Chief among these is the artistic choice of words. A true poet uses words to suggest as much as to describe. He may use proper names which are musical in themselves —

> Usumcasane and Theridamas.
> From Arachosia, from Candaor east,
> And Margiana to the Hyrcanian cliffs
> Of Caucasus, and dark Iberian dales.

or which, in addition, call up great memories

> Rich Mexico, the seat of Montezume.

He will always seek the new and vivid phrase instead of the outworn and colourless. Today we have *the man in blue, needless to say, the festive occasion,* and a hundred other tags, the avoidance of which is the aim of every careful writer. It is the neglect of this principle which spoils much eighteenth-century work. The *swain,* the *fair sex,* the *finny tribe,* the *conscious look* — these and a thousand other expressions recur over and over again; they are a main constituent of pseudo-classic diction.

Conversely, the romantic poets — Wordsworth, Keats, and Tennyson especially — over and over again achieve the magic phrase, the key which opens the door into another world —

> Magic casements, opening on the foam
> Of perilous seas, in faery lands forlorn.

Old, forgotten, far-off things and battles long ago.

The light that never was on sea or land,
The inspiration and the poet's dream.

Fretted to dulcet jars
And silvern chatter the pale ports o' the moon.

34. These "jewels five words long" defy analysis; we cannot say *why* they affect us. But that is not the case with all fine phrases. Often, if we examine our emotions carefully, we find that an expression is full of suggestiveness. This, as we have seen, is often due to the use of a peculiarly pregnant metaphor; but it may, too, arise where there is no figure of speech, merely as a result of the choice of words. Turn back to the first chapter, and read again the passage from Thackeray and the bungler's imitation of it, and you will realise how large a part is played by this rightness of atmosphere in words.

35. There are, too, less subtle kinds of suggestion — the use of colour words, for instance.

Some of us are bad visualists; the poet may describe meadows and lakes, mountains and oceans, but we cannot see them; the novelist may tell us exactly in what corner of his hero's attic his broken-legged chair stood, but we have no clear mental picture — we could not say whether it was a Windsor chair or a rush-seated one. But colours are so vivid and so simple that the dullest of us cannot say "green" without a bright green haze before his inner eye. Colour words, then, change a drab poem into brightness. The skilful poet will avoid clashing colours as carefully as an artist. He will not say —

And in one hand she held
Pink dahlias, scarlet poppies, marigolds
Of orange-yellow, while the other raised
Lightly her sky-blue skirt with flounces green.

You will find it an interesting task to discover the favourite colours of poets. Tennyson loves the brighter hues —

A million emeralds break from the ruby-budded lime.

Spenser has a fondness for contrasts of sun and shadow — black against yellow or white; Shelley weaves a rainbow from iridescent moonbeams.

36. Other things, too, there are in style — the balance and proportion which avoid monotony and exaggeration, the close observation and faithful portrayal of nature, of material objects, of the thoughts and passions of men, the attitude of mind which sees life as a vale of tears or a dream, a huge joke or a meaningless riddle; the subjectivity of the writer who identifies himself with what he describes; the objectivity of the writer who, cold and detached, draws his characters from the outside. But these are more individual matters; they border upon the Holy of Holies of style — personality. We can discover an author's mannerisms, and note that Hardy has a fondness for the verb "to lip," that Keats shows a preference for *lush* and such formations as *palely;* that Shelley likes hoary-headed youths, *inane* (as a noun), *daedal,* and *intense;* but when we have done all we can in this way, we have not reached the inner shrine.

EXERCISE II

1. Study the following passages carefully. Write an appreciation of the use in each of repetition, stating exactly what effect is produced —

(*a*) Work! work! work! till the cocks are crowing aloof,
Work! work! work! till the stars shine through the roof,
And it's Oh! to be a slave in the land of the barbarous Turk
Where woman has never a soul to save, if this be Christian work!

Hood : The Song of *the Shirt.*

(*b*) Where are the songs of Spring? Ay, where are they ?
Think not of them, thou hast thy music too.

Keats : *Ode to Autumn.*

(*c*) O slowly, slowly rase she up,
And slowly put she on;

And slowly rade she out the way
Wi' mony a weary groan.

The Queen's Marie.

(*d*) I saw pale kings and princes too,
Pale warriors, death-pale were they all.

Keats : *La Belle Dame Sans Merci.*

(*e*) Blow, bugle, blow, set the wild echoes flying,
Blow, bugle; answer, echoes, dying, dying, dying.

Tennyson : *The Princess.*

(*f*) Stop him! stop him! murder! thief! fire —
Stop fire stop fire! — Oh, Sir Anthony — call! call!
bid'm stop! murder! fire!

Sheridan : *The Rivals.*

2. Write a half-dozen or so lines of verse (any metre) or prose, using repetition to express (*a*) delight in the prospect of rest, (*b*) distaste for study, (*c*) love of the open air, (*d*) grief at the death of a favourite dog.

3. Discuss the use of similarity (including all forms of repetition) and contrast in the following :

(*a*) And the whirr of their wayfaring thinned
And surceased on the sky.

Hardy : *The Souls of the Slain.*

(*b*) I fear thee, ancient Mariner!
I fear thy skinny hand!
And thou art long and lank and brown,
As is the ribb'd sea-sand....
I fear thee and thy glittering eye,
And thy skinny band so brown.

Coleridge : *The Ancient Mariner.*

(*c*) My mother bore me in the southern wild,
And I am black, but O, my soul is white!
White as an angel is the English child,
But I am black, as if bereaved of light.

Blake : *The Little Black Boy.*

(*d*) Calm and deep peace in this wide air,
These leaves that redden to the fall;
And in my heart, if calm at all,
If any calm, a calm despair.

Tennyson : *In Memoriam.*

(*e*) The gray sea and the long black land;
And the yellow half-moon large and low.

Browning : *Meeting at Night.*

(*f*) A foreground black with stones and slags,
Beyond, a line of heights, and higher
All barr'd with long white cloud the scornful crags,
And highest, snow and fire.

Tennyson : *The Palace of Art.*

(*g*) Peace, peace! he is not dead, he doth not sleep —
He hath awakened from the dream of life.

Shelley : *Adonais.*

4. Comment upon the choice of words and ideas in the following :

(*a*) And I heard the waters wagging in a long ironic
laughter.

Hardy : *The Voice of Things.*

(*b*) Belovëd, I am quickly out of sight.
I pray that you will love more than my dust.

Meredith : *Vittoria.*

(*c*) Our noisy years seem moments in the being
Of the eternal Silence.

Wordsworth : *Ode on Intimations of Immortality.*

(*d*) The loftiest star of unascended heaven
Pinnacled dim in the intense inane.

Shelley : *Prometheus Unbound.*

(*e*) Finish, good lady; the bright day is done,
And we are for the dark.

Shakespeare : *Antony and Cleopatra.*

(*f*) Some of our descendants may see the chimney-pots as rich a purple as the mountain peaks, and find the lamp-posts as old and natural as the trees. — Chesterton : *The Defendant.*

(*g*) If there be a regal solitude, it is a sick bed. How the patient lords it there! ... He changes *sides* oftener than a politician. Now he lies full length, then half-length, obliquely, transversely, head and feet quite across the bed; and none accuses him of tergiversation.

Lamb : *The Convalescent.*

(*h*) Listening now to the tide in its broad-flung shipwrecking roar,
Now to the scream of a madden'd beach dragg'd down by the wave.

Tennyson : *Maud.*

(*i*) I warm'd both hands before the fire of life;
It sinks, and I am ready to depart.

Landor.

5. Discuss the use of simile and metaphor in the following passages, saying whether the figure is appropriate, and mentioning what fresh ideas it suggests. In each case write down a simile or metaphor to suggest another aspect of the same subject.

(*a*) From the fixt lull of Heaven, she saw
Time, like a pulse, shake fierce
Through all the worlds.

Rossetti : *The Blessed Damosel.*

(*b*) And the tumbling billows like leap-frog came,
Each over the other's back.

Hood : *The Mermaid of Margate.*

(*c*) Thoughts black as death
Like a stirred pool in sunshine break.

Meredith : *Modern Love.*

(*d*) Suspicions amongst thoughts are like bats amongst birds — they ever fly by twilight.

Bacon : *Of Suspicion.*

(*e*) There is no antidote against the opium of time.

Sir T. Browne : *Urn-Burial.*

(*f*) The paths of glory lead but to the grave.

Gray : *Elegy written in a Country Churchyard.*

(*g*) The primrose way to the everlasting bonfire.

Shakespeare : *Macbeth.*

(*h*) That inverted Bowl we call The Sky.

FitzGerald : *The Rubaíyát of Omar Khayyám.*

(*i*) She had no imagination about anybody's life save on the side she bumped against.

H. James : *The Spoils of Poynton.*

6. Quote lines making generous use of the following sounds : (i) *l*, (ii) *s*, (iii) *m*, (iv) *p*. In each case state what idea the sound suggests.

7. Draw up a, sound-scheme of the following, and discuss its suitability to the ideas expressed :

(*a*) Heard melodies are sweet, but those unheard
Are sweeter; therefore, ye soft pipes, play on;
Not to the sensual ear, but, more endear'd,
Pipe to the spirit ditties of no tone.

Keats : *Ode on a Grecian Urn.*

(*b*) All things have rest, and ripen toward the grave
In silence; ripen, fall, and cease :
Give us long rest or death, dark death, or dreamful
ease.

Tennyson : *The Lotus-Eaters.*

(*c*) From maniac laughter to piercing lamentation, there was not a single note of human anguish of which he was not master.

Macaulay : *Moore's Life of Lord Byron.*

8. Write a detailed appreciation of the metre of the following :

(*a*) Milton's sonnet on the Massacre of the Piedmontese, (*b*) Keats's *La Belle Dame Sans Merci, (c)* Wordsworth's *Ode*

On the intimations of immortality, (*d*) Portia's speech in praise of mercy (*e*) Shelley's *Adonais*, (*f*) Tennyson's *Lotus-Eaters*, (*g*) *Browning's Home Thoughts from Abroad*, (*h*) Arnold's *Requiescat*.

9. Criticise the rime scheme in (*a*) Wordsworth's *We are Seven*, (*b*) Coleridge's *Ancient Mariner*, (*c*) Tennyson's *Lady of Shalott*.

10. Write down six phrases which seem to you particularly happy; and say, if you can, why you like them.

11. Read Tennyson's *The Palace of Art* : add (in prose or, preferably, in Tennyson's metre) another arras-picture.

12. Give examples of true and false personification, giving reasons for your classification.

13. Write down the ideas suggested to you by each of the following similes or metaphors :

(*a*) Back on herself her serpent pride had curl'd.

Tennyson : *The Palace of Art*.

(*b*) Those dragon eyes of anger'd Eleanor
Do hunt me, day and night.

Tennyson : *A Dream of Fair Women*.

(*c*) All our yesterdays have lighted fools
The way to dusty death.

Shakespeare : *Macbeth*.

(*d*) Dawn's Left Hand was in the Sky.

Omar Khayyám : *Rubaíyát*.

(*e*) One Moment in Annihilation's Waste,
One Moment, of the Well of Life to taste.

Omar Khayyám : *Rubaíyát*.

(*f*) In the fire of Spring
The Winter garment of Repentance fling.

Omar Khayyám : *Rubaíyát*.

(g) Bright else, and fast, the stream of life may roll,...

Yet each will have one anguish — his own soul
Which perishes of cold.

Arnold : *Progress.*

(*h*) The soul of Adonais, like a star,
Beacons from the abode where the Eternal are.

Shelley : *Adonais.*

(*i*) Life's a single pilgrim,
Fighting unarmed amongst a thousand soldiers.

Beddoes : *The Fool's Tragedy.*

14. Write down metaphors expressing some of the qualities of a house, a child, a whale, sleep, death, expectancy, a cuckoo, time.

15. Make a detailed study of *L'Allegro* and *Il Penseroso*, writing down in two columns all the direct contrasts you can find.

16. "Awry and doubled up are his gray bones" (Hardy). Give six other instances of the felicitous use of a colour word.

17. Rewrite as a chapter in a novel the account of Margaret's meeting with Henry of Cranstoun in Canto III. of Scott's *Lay of the Last Minstrel.*

18. Examine carefully some metaphors and similes of (*a*) Shelley, (*b*) Tennyson, (*c*) Dickens, and see what you can gather from them as to the interests, aim, and outlook of each writer. Which most frequently uses as material the common-place things of life such as kettles and doorknobs? Which shows the closest acquaintance with Nature? Which is most concerned with the abstract and the unsubstantial?

19. Write two contrasted pieces of prose or verse, one on Summer and one on Winter.

3

The Varieties of Style

37. The varieties of style are infinite; all that can be attempted here is to give a brief account of the main groups into which they can be divided, and this can best be done by a rough chronological survey.

It must not, of course, be imagined that one style ever "succeeds" another as night succeeds day in the tropics — "with one stride." Fashions in style, as in dress, change gradually; the new and the old overlap, and there are always some who do not follow the fashion at all. But, however slowly and uncertainly, style does change: any well-read person of average intelligence, given a passage he has never seen before, can guess within a hundred years when it was written.

The Simple-Sentence Style

38. The most primitive style in the world is the simple-sentence style. Young children use nothing else — "And I met Johnny; and Johnny has a new Teddy; and it squeaks; and he wants me to go to tea with him; and may I, please ?" Each idea is given equal prominence, because each is expressed as it arises, without any attempt to connect it formally with what precedes. Now turn to *Genesis* :

> And God set them in the firmament of the heaven, to give light upon the earth, and to rule over the day and over the night, and to divide the light from the darkness.

So, too, in the *Anglo-Saxon Chronicle* (tenth century) :

> At this time Ethelbald the king died. And his body lies

> at Sherborne. And Ethelbright his brother succeeded to all that kingdom. And in his day a great harrying fleet came up and destroyed Winchester, and Osric the alderman with the men of Hampshire fought against the horde.

And in Malory (fifteenth century) :

> Thenne Syr Bedwere departed and wente to the swerde and lyghtly took hit up, and wente to the water syde and there he bounde the gyrdyl aboute the hyltes, and thenne he threwe the swerde as farre in to the water as he myght, and there cam an arme and an bande above the water and mette it, and caught it, and so shoke it thryse, and braundysshed and then vanysshed awaye the hande wyth the swerde in the water.

Later use of Simple-Sentences Type

Wherever men *begin* to write, they use this style — a style with the minimum of dependent clauses, a style simple and straightforward, each idea being linked with the preceding by *and* or some equivalent.

39. But it would not be true to say that, only the childlike men of early civilisations use it. You will find it in Defoe (1661-1731) :

> I understood him in many things, and let him know I was very well pleased with him; in a little while I began to speak to him and teach him to speak to me; and first, I made him know his name should be Friday, which was the day I saved his life, and I called him so for the memory of the time; I likewise taught him to say master, and then let him know that was to be my name; I likewise taught him to say yes and no, and to know the meaning of them.

in Tennyson :

> The steer fell down at the plow and the harvest died from
> the field,

And the men dropt dead in the valleys and half of the
cattle went lame,
And the roof sank in on the hearth, and the dwelling broke
into flame;
And the shouting of these wild birds ran into the hearts of
my crew.

in Morris, in Coleridge, in Dickens, in almost all imaginative writing. Why? Because it is the only style which can produce certain effects — naïve simplicity; mediaeval romanticism; plain, direct and vivid narrative; that return to the short, simple sentences of our youth which arises from intense emotion.

40. There is, however, a considerable difference between the sometimes awkward simplicity of the unpractised hand and the highly wrought simplicity of the finished artist. No one could mistake the first of the above passages for the work of a modern writer; no one would imagine that the last was written by a beginner.

The Detailed Style

41. The very earliest prose makes little use of detail; when an author has to express his ideas laboriously in a language not yet suppled by use for artistic purposes and with fingers unaccustomed to writing, he is content with the more important facts. Indeed, it is probable that, in this early stage of civilisation, he has not learnt to observe minutely: if he describes a battle, he has little to say except that sword dashed against shield and clove the helmets of those doomed to die, while the black raven hovered above.

But at a rather later stage, when the resources of the language have been explored by pioneers and the writer has ready to his hand a whole host of phrases, we find an extreme fondness for detail and, too often, a lack of discrimination in its choice. The poet, with a child's fresh delight in everything, will stop his story to give us a full description of the heroine's dress or the various joints into which the hero divided the deer he had just shot.

The artist who understands his craft knows that a superfluity of irrelevant detail is worse than no detail at all, but the tyro cannot understand that what interests him may bore us. Even Chaucer sometimes sins, though he generally offers a handsome apology! Spenser, coming after changes in the language had thrown back the art of literature almost to the beginning again, has scarcely a glimmering notion of this principle. Any stanza in the *Faery Queene* is beautiful; but after we have read ten descriptions of the scenery through which the Knight is passing, we grow a little wearied even of beauty.

Later uses of detailed Style

42. Given a sense of proportion in the writer, the love of detail is, of course, an advantage. In the hands of Shakespeare and Keats, Gibbon and Macaulay, Tennyson and Rossetti, it adds colour and body without being carried, save in rare cases, to the point of exaggeration. Keats's *St. Agnes' Eve* would lose all its beauty if it were stripped of its detailed descriptions. For this exuberant delight in small things is of the very stuff of English romanticism — and romanticism sits more easily on our race than classicism. Whenever the nation has renewed its youth, has looked out upon the world with a fresh zest — as in the great Renaissance which culminated under Elizabeth, the romantic revival of the late eighteenth century, the Pre-Raphaelite movement — we find again the concrete rather than the abstract style, the detailed rather than the general.

The Exuberant Style

43. The mediaeval love of detail, like its Renaissance counterpart, often goes with a love of words for their own sake. The pleasure of Skelton (1460 ?-1529) as he piles synonym upon synonym :

> Tattered and jagged
> Rudely rayne beaten,
> Rusty and moughte eaten

the gusto with which Nash ascribes virtue after virtue to the herring, the relish with which Marlowe rolls off proper names,

the joy with which Keats, like Spenser before him, resuscitates old words and invents new seem to us more closely akin to 'Rabelais'[1] zest than are the wearisome "lists" in mediaeval poets; but the same spirit informs them all : it is only mastery of the instrument — and our familiarity with the language — that varies.

Use of Tags

44. Another result of this inadequate command of language is the use of stock phrases, little tags — often almost meaningless — to fill up a line or make a rime. When the poet was a minstrel who recited without a manuscript, it is obvious that he would welcome these bits of mechanical speech : while he was saying "I gesse" or "withouten doute," he could be recalling or composing the next line. When the poet ceased to be a minstrel, he still followed the bad tradition.

Ballad Style

45. Perhaps it is the ballad which makes the most lavish use of these conventional fragments, for the literary value of the ballad more than that of any other mediaeval verse form lay in story and situation rather than nicety of expression. For this reason and because of its early connection with dancing, the ballad seems to us the quintessence of mediaeval naïveté. We find, for instance, the peculiar indirectness of statement :

> She hadna been about the King's court
> A month, but barely three.

the continual use of repetition in phrase and incident :

> O cherry, cherry was her cheek...
> And coral, coral was her lips.

the preference of monologue and dialogue to reported speech and, often, to reported action — *Edward, Edward* is dialogue pure and simple; the use of conventional epithets — *bonny son,*

1. Himself (1483-1553) mediaeval in time, as we count the middle ages in the history of English literature, but Renaissance in spirit and caught in the full tide of the French Renaissance.

gowden locks, noble lord; the rough but vigorous lilt of the ballad metre; the apparent determination to tell everything in the longest possible way, so that, if the hero bids farewell to his wife, his mother, his son, and his two daughters, he does it in five stanzas, almost identical except for the proper names.

All these characteristics make the ballad seem so full of marked oddities that there is little wonder that eighteenth century poets thought ballad-forging the easiest of tasks — little wonder, too, that they proved mistaken. For these are but the external signs; the ballad spirit itself is something more intangible — something at once very young and very old in outlook, simple and sophisticated, like a child trying to imitate a worldly-minded elder, a spirit infinitely far removed from the common-sense, no-nonsense-about-*us* attitude of the Augustan school of Pope.

You are unlikely to read much outside the styles already treated until you reach the Elizabethan period itself, and here you meet not one style but many. Literature, like all the other sides of life, is reborn, looks out upon the world with fresh eyes and, like all young things, is anxious to try experiments.

This is not to say that there were no conventions in verse; much Elizabethan verse is even more conventional than the worst mediaeval allegories with their bloodless personifications of incredibly dull virtues and — still more serious, since they provided the comic relief — incredibly dull vices. But the conventions were different. Spenser, it is true, follows the old tradition; but he fills the old bottles with new wine. He may imagine that his wine is the same as that of the old allegorists — unmatured didacticism, moral edification — but in reality it is the love of all bright and beautiful things. It says much, indeed, for the low ebb to which poetry had sunk, that of the first two great Elizabethan poets one felt the need of writing an elaborate *Defence of Poetry,* and the other felt bound to invent a moral purpose for his pictures of fair maids and bold knights.

Spenserian or Simple Aesthetic

46. For the Spenserian style is the style of a lover of beautiful sights and sounds, rather than that of a thinker of profound thoughts. Take a typical stanza from the *Faerie Queene* :

The sight of whom, though now decayed and mard,
And eke but hardly seene by candle-light,
Yet, like a Diamond of rich regard,
In doubtfull shadow of the darksome night
With starrie beames about her shining bright,
These marchants fixed eyes did so amaze,
That what through wonder, and what through delight,
A while on her they greedily did gaze,
And did her greatly like, and did her greatly praize.

Here what first strikes us is the easy, unhasting, untiring pace — a pace largely due to the metre. The stanza-form flows on, rime answering and anticipating rime, so that there seems no natural stopping place until we reach the slight backward swirl and pause of the last line. What a contrast with the heroic-couplet of Pope, a form where at the end of every two lines we seem to have reached the end of the poem! But the stanza-form is not alone responsible for the dallying sweetness of the verse : take a few other lines in the same metre :

The cock upon the barn-door stretched and crowed.
The herd-boy in the stable cursed and swore.
Far in the east the dawn's first redness glowed.
The milkmaid shivered at the frosty door.
The air was dank, and grey, and thick and frore.

There is no gentle reverie in that the sounds are harsh; the clauses are short; the lines are end-stopped; in an unskilful hand, the verse-form has lost all its characteristic beauties. Spenser's work is the reverse of all this; his whole stanza is a single sentence, in which clause melts gently into clause, words glide gently along to form a slow succession of lovely but not striking pictures. The nearest approach to that abrupt use of contrast which constitutes the striking is, as generally in Spenser, the juxtaposition of light and darkness — *doubtfull shadow, darksome night* on the one hand; *candle-light, diamond,* and *starrie beams* on the other. It is true that Spenser can, when he pleases, paint the grotesque and the horrible; but he so seldom pleases, that his name is always associated with a style full of languorous loveliness.

Thomson, in *The Castle of Indolence,* and Keats are the best-known among those who have learnt Spenser's lesson. Shelley, in *The Revolt of Islam* and *Adonais,* never quite succeeds in catching Spenser's urbane leisureliness — he has too ardent a spirit; Tennyson, though he often *(e.g.* in *The Palace of Art)* captures Spenser's grace, does not use his metre and has a deeper note; Byron, in *Childe Harold,* by staccato sentences, and an entire lack of Spenser's melody, changes the whole nature of the stanza. For the Spenserian style is the idyllic style, and Spenser is our greater and more Romantic André Chénier — but the André Chénier of the *Idylls,* not that of the *Iambes;* a solemn ecstasy is Spenser's nearest approach to passion.

This lack of passion, this steady contemplation of beauty, this careful artistry was apparently regarded by the Elizabethans as the "correct thing" in verse. Sometimes, as in Marlowe's *Hero and Leander* and Shakespeare's *Venus and Adonis* and *Lucrece,* the dramatist warmed the poet to something more than mere lazy delight in beauty; but the most impassioned lines in the most impassioned poems are cold and artificial beside the human anguish or joy of *Lear* and Middleton's *Changeling,* of Webster's *Duchess of Malfi* and Heywood's *A Woman Killed with Kindness* — or even of Marlowe's *Tamburlaine.*

Conventional Amorist Style

47. The Elizabethan sonneteers adopt another style — the conventional amorist. Some of them go so far as to borrow both sentiments and phrasing from foreign poets; nearly all of them address similar calmly perfervid appeals to similar inexorable mistresses. The lady's eyes are always stars, her cheeks always roses, her lips always cherries. This is not to say that the resulting poem is bad; often it is a little gem of dainty melody. But its pretence at passion never pretends to be more than a pretence.

In various forms the conventional amorist style is found throughout civilised literature: flirting, the game of making love, is a time-honoured amusement for spare moments; and when once poetry comes to be written by and for those classes which, having abundant leisure, invent a graceful art of love-making, the languishing lover, or his counterpart the gay Lothario, becomes a common figure in verse. Sidney and Campion, Wither and Herrick, Carew and Suckling, even grim Ben Jonson and the savage Landor bring out their lyres and serenade.

"Conceited" Style

48. But at different times the style takes rather different forms. With the Elizabethans it is generally "conceited," that is to say, a figure of speech, or "conceit," is twisted and turned and squeezed till the last drop of sense is extracted. Thomas Campion's "There is a garden in her face " is a case in point. Here the lady's garden (roses and lilies, with cherry lips) is paradise, while her eyes are the angels keeping guard, and her brows, in lieu of a flaming sword, are bows to kill intruders who would touch the cherries.

"Conceits" were not, of course, confined to love-poems : they are found almost everywhere in Elizabethan verse; Shakespeare's early plays, especially *Richard II*, are full of them. But they are most noticeable in the love-poems just because there material was scanty, and the same old notions did duty over and over again. This at length became evident even to the poets themselves, and, by a natural development, we get the Metaphysical Style, which can be said to begin, with Donne's manuscript poems, about 1590, and dragged on a discredited existence till after the Restoration.

Metaphysical Style

49. The ordinary metaphors and similes had become commonplaces; they were to the man with an imagination what plain, unfigurative speech is to us. When he felt truly poetical, his mind "jumped off." from the ordinary analogies and comparisons to something more remote. Common men could see that Lucasta's cheek was like a rose; your Metaphysical saw in it the red oriflamme of war, that war in which eyes shot arrows at the vanquished swain. For the "conceited" amorist, Celia's eyes might be daggers; for the metaphysical their rays were knitting-needles, weaving the web of men's fate. At his best, the meta-physical poet is sublimely daring, witness Donne's —

> Those great fore-fathers of the Church that saw
> More in the cloud than we in fire;

at his worst, he is absurd, witness the same poet's —

> Hither with crystal vials, lovers, come
> And take my tears, which are Love's wine,
> And try your mistress' tears at home;
> For all are false, that taste not just like mine.

For the weakness of the metaphysical poet was that, when his imagination failed to work, he used his ingenuity instead. And if even a great poet like Donne often sinned, it was only to be expected that the lesser poets — writers without his imagination and without his passion — would copy his worst points and produce a series of cold and ridiculous attempts to surprise.

This is what happened. As we have seen, the value of simile and metaphor consists largely in a nice balance of contrast and similarity. "Behold we put bits in the horses' mouths.... But the tongue can no man tame." Here the surprise evoked by the idea of taming a tongue is succeeded by an instantaneous perception that, though horses and tongues seem utterly unlike, there is real similarity between an unbridled horse and an unbridled tongue. The greater the initial sense of incongruity, the more striking the metaphor. But the Metaphysicals too often overload one scale of the balance : the surprise is not followed by a feeling of essential likeness; we feel that such alikeness as there may be is forced and superficial.

The Hyperbolic Style

This extravagance in language, then, lacks the charm of the earlier Elizabethan excesses, because it is less spontaneous. Shakespeare's younger contemporaries had the adolescent tendency to gush and exaggerate, and to this tendency they gave free play in the drama; life to them was so splendid and so strange that even the most "high, astounding terms" were inadequate to express what they felt. Beginning with Marlowe and Kyd, this hyperbolic style remains characteristic of Elizabethan drama to the end. Whenever the dramatist wishes to be particularly impressive, he becomes magniloquent, with a magniloquence sometimes gloriously successful, sometimes perilously near rant. It is not merely Marlowe's :

Techelles, draw thy sword,
And wound the earth, that it may cleave in twain,
And we descend into th' infernal vaults
To hale the Fatal Sisters by the hair;

it is Shakespeare's :

Heaven's cherubim, horsed
Upon the sightless couriers of the air,
Shall blow the horrid deed in every eye,
That tears shall drown the wind.

In truth the Elizabethans had re-discovered the possibilities of language : it is for them no longer a mere mechanical means for the expression of ideas; it is clay to be modelled into quaint shapes, a toy to be played with.

Euphuism

50. This is as evident in prose as in verse. We get Euphuism (c. 1579-1600) with its elaborate cross-alliteration, its plays on words, its antitheses, its mechanically balanced sentences, its endless comparisons drawn from "unnatural natural history" :

Though Aeneas were too *f*ickle to Dido, yet Troylus was too *f*aithfull to Cressida : though others seem counterfeit in their *d*eeds, yet, Lucilla, persuade

> yourself, that Euphues will be always current in his *d*ealings.

Arcadianism

51. About the same time we get Arcadianism, with its rather laboured elegance, its compound words, its comparisons of the natural to the artificial (*e.g.* night likened to black velvet), its idyllic pastoralism :

> "There were...meadows enamelled with all sorts of eye-pleasing flowers; thickets which, being lined with most pleasant shade, were witnessed so to by the cheerful disposition of many well-tuned birds; each pasture stored with sheep, feeding with sober security, while the pretty lambs with bleating oratory craved the dams' comfort.

The Pregnant or Epigrammatic Style

52. Bacon could and did write (in *The New Atlantis* and elsewhere) a clear unadorned style, but in his essays he, too, shows the Elizabethan tendency to play with — and upon — words. Not, of course, that he is guilty of the eccentricities of Lyly and Sidney. His main characteristics are a laconic brevity, a stately harmony, a full mind, a free use of antithesis, of "conceits," and an abruptness which does not attempt to make a natural transition from one idea to another. Consider, for instance :

> For envy is a gadding passion, anct walketh the streets, and doth not keep home; *Non est curiosus, quin idem sit malevolus.*[2]

> Men of noble birth are noted to be envious towards new men when they rise. For the distance is altered : and it is like a deceit of the eye that, when others come on, they think themselves go back.

---

2. There is no busybody that is not evil-disposed.

Fantastic Prose

53. This epigrammatic style was taken up and modified by the writers of Characters (1614 and on), who suppled it, gave it a more familiar tone, and increased the number and audacity of the conceits, until they came to write what may almost be called metaphysical prose. Thus in Earle we find :

> A gallant is one that was born and shapt for his cloathes : and if *Adam* had not falne, had liu'd to no purpose....
>
> *A Cooke* : The Kitchen is his Hell and hee the Divell in it, where his meate and he frye together.

Architectural Prose

Alongside these and other quaint styles ran an undercurrent of less eccentric prose. One stream in this undercurrent was a prose which in vocabulary and in sentence structure owed a great deal to Bacon, but more to Latin, — the architectural prose. Here the writer used his words to build great arches and pinnacles of sound. Milton's prose — though Milton often left half-built ruins — was of this order; so was Browne's.

But Browne had in addition much of the subtlety of thought, the odd imagination of the best metaphysical poets. Note in the following the short epigrammatic sentences at first, changing to the steady roll of the trumpet-and-drum peroration :

> Afflictions induce callosities; miseries are slippery or fall like snow upon us, which notwithstanding is no unhappy stupidity. To be ignorant of evils to come, and forgetful of evils past, is a merciful provision in nature, whereby we digest the mixture of our few and evil days, and, our delivered senses not relapsing into cutting remembrances, our sorrows are not kept raw by the edge of repetitions.... There is nothing strictly immortal, but immortality. Whatever hath no beginning may be confident of no end; — which is the peculiar of that necessary essence that cannot destroy itself : all

> others have a dependent being and within the reach of destruction.... But man is a noble animal, splendid in ashes, and pompous in the grave, solemnizing nativities and deaths with equal lustre, nor omitting ceremonies of bravery in the infamy of his nature.

54. Poetry then had become wildly figurative and fantastic; prose had become a kind of unmetrical poetry : the inevitable reaction came. But reaction in art is not the stopping and reversing of an engine : it is the flowing and ebbing of a tide. There is a period of confusion when the tide is on the turn, and, even long before the "turn" itself, there are undercurrents flowing seawards. So the revolt against elaboration and the striving after simplicity is evident here and there long before the Restoration of 1660, just as isolated instances of the old style can be found years after it. But the Restoration may be considered the "turn."

The Plain Style

55. There are several varieties of the Restoration plain style. There is the limpid ease of Waller :

> Tobacco is the worst of things, which they
> To English landlords, as their tribute, pay.
> Such is the mould that the bless'd tenant feeds
> On precious fruits, and pays his rent in weeds.

Dryden's verse, masculine and sonorous, often antithetical :

> Panting and pensive now she ranged alone,
> And wandered in the kingdoms once her own.
> The common hunt, though from their rage restrained
> By sovereign power, her company disdained,
> Grinned as they passed, and with a glaring eye
> Gave gloomy signs of secret enmity.

the gentlemanly style of his prose, full of a cultured common-sense and an easy mastery of the language :

> But enough of this; there is such a variety of game springing up before me, that I am distracted in my choice, and know not which to follow. 'Tis sufficient

> to say, according to the proverb, that *here is God's plenty.* We have our forefathers and great-granddames all before us, as they were in Chaucer's days.

the racy, familiar, imaginative prose of Bunyan :

> After that, he went to the iron gate, for that must be opened too. But that lock went damnably hard; yet the key did open it. Then they thrust open the gate to make their escape with speed; but that gate as it opened made such a creaking that it waked Giant Despair, who, hastily rising to pursue his prisoners, felt his limbs to fail, for his fits took him again, so that he could by no means go after them.

Miltonic Grand Style

56. There is, too, Milton's Grand Style itself, which — though not simple — has the severity and finished outline of Greek architecture. Let us take a short passage in illustration :

> So spake the Enemy of Mankind, enclosed
> In serpent, inmate bad, and toward Eve
> Addressed his way — not with indented wave,
> Prone on the ground, as since, but on his rear,
> Circular base of rising folds, that towered
> Fold above fold a surging maze, his head
> Crested aloft, and carbuncle his eyes;
> With burnished neck of verdant gold, erect
> Amidst his circling spires, that on the grass
> Floated redundant : pleasing was his shape
> And lovely, never since of serpent-kind
> Lovelier.

First, you will notice that he has learnt from Spenser the use of the sentence-paragraph, but that his sentence-paragraph is not, like Spenser's sentence-stanza, a loose-jointed ambling pad : it is a war-horse trained to turn at the least pull of the rein, always stately, always full of fire. Note, too, the variety of pause — a variety partly learnt from the Elizabethan drama in its best days, partly due to his classical studies, but largely the result of his own genius.

Perhaps next thing observed will be Milton's fondness for Latin-derived words — *addressed, indented, prone, redundant* — often used in their classical sense rather than in the sense they bear in English. In Milton's hands this adds dignity to the verse, but it is a dangerous method for minor poets, who may easily fall into such depths of bathos as :

> Others, destitute
> Of real zeal, to every altar bend
> By lucre sway'd, and act the basest things
> To be styl'd honourable.

Another "trick" of Milton is the "inverted epithet," or the adjective placed after the noun — *inmate bad.* Often, too, he will balance his noun between two adjectives — *faded splendour wan.*

All these, of course, are the mere externals of Milton, valuable chiefly because they are the natural expression of his mind. In the eighteenth century there arose a Milton craze; dozens of men who had nothing of the Miltonic mind caught the Miltonic mannerisms. The result was verse full of heavy pomposities, but empty of sublimity, a David strutting round in Saul's armour. Yet, though the poets who wrote Miltonic epics on cider-making or hunting seem ridiculous to us, the revival of interest in the Grand Style influenced for good such poets as Gray and Collins, bringing back to poetry the loftiness of thought, imagery, and diction which it had lost in the age of Pope.

The Later Plain Style

57. For simplicity, ease, and wit were soon divorced from the force, breadth of outlook, and dignity to which they were wedded in Dryden. Dryden commanded many metres and a multitude of rhythmical effects; Pope, and still more his followers, were never quite at home away from the heroic couplet, and even on that instrument they could play only a few tunes —

tunes, too, lacking in orchestration and thin in melody, though at their best delicate and neatly finished. Satirical and semi-satirical matter, too, became more and more popular, the feline softness and sharpness of Pope's couplet being as well suited to his rather hysterical spite as the vigour of Dryden's couplet had been suited to his downright blows and good-humoured contempt.

The same thing was evident in prose. To Dryden's school of sturdy, common-sense, plain English succeeded a still plainer style — the style of Swift. Alongside this was the style of Addison, a style intended for an audience largely composed of "gentlewomen," and coloured throughout by a "gentlewomanly" familiarity and delicacy. In Addison's own hands the effect was delightful; but what in him was a finished artist's ideal of cultured "chat" became in careless hands a prose marked by all the faults of uncultured colloquialism. Sentence-structure became slipshod, vocabulary unselected, grammatical accuracy itself was neglected, and the conception of the sentence as a phrase in prose-music was entirely lost. All this is not generally true of the greater writers, such as Fielding and Sterne; but it is true of the mass of controversial and periodical writing.

Johnsonese

58. Then, as always, the law of contrast acted again; and we get the Johnsonian style. The Doctor, sturdy classicist as he was, had read widely among the Elizabethans and Jacobeans, and Browne was one of his favourite writers. From Browne and from his own Latin studies, as well no doubt as from the reaction against the prevailing meanness of diction, he caught a fondness for Latin words — the *-osities* and *-ations* which have been so much ridiculed; from Browne and the classics, again, he drew a preference for sentences with a definite rhythmic flow. Unfortunately, the Doctor's ear was not very sensitive, and had, in addition, become too much accustomed to the regular rise and fall of the Popian antithesis and the Popian couplet. So it came to pass that his style was apt to be mechanically balanced and, like himself, rather heavy. But, except when it became a caricature of itself, it was nervous, manly, and forcible, rhetorical in the best sense. Even at its worst, it was a corrective to the prevailing faults of the age.

A characteristic piece of Addison set cheek by jowl with a characteristic piece of Johnson will show how far the pendulum had swung :

> He then renewed his attention, and, from time to time, fell a praising the widow. He made, indeed a mistake as to one of her pages, whom at his first entering he took for Astyanax; but quickly set himself right in the particular, though, at the same time, he owned he should have been very glad to have seen the little boy, who, says he, must needs be a very line child by the account that is given of him.

> Thus, some make comedy a representation of mean, and others of bad men; some think that its essence consists in the unimportance, others in the fictitiousness of the transaction. But any man's reflections will inform him, that every dramatic composition which raises mirth is comic; and that, to raise mirth, it is by no means universally necessary that the personages should be either mean or corrupt, nor always requisite that the action should be trivial, nor even that it should be fictitious.

Dr. Johnson was not, of course, the sole early representative of the reaction — Burke brought back some of the old wild audacity of imagination; Gibbon, who owed not a little to Johnson, brought a certain gorgeousness of diction and rhythm and more than the old fullness of thought and learning — but Johnson was by far the most influential. He remained the Dictator in letters, at least as far as Academies for Young Ladies were concerned, till well on into the next century; even Scott not infrequently falls into the veriest Johnsonese, and Macaulay owes most of his characteristic virtues as well as most of his characteristic faults to the Doctor.

Whimsical Style

59. By the time Scott died, however, English prose had almost achieved the infinite variety of the Elizabethan period. There was the whimsical style of Lamb, which owed something to many writers — especially to Browne — but yet remained intensely original, allusive, humorous, pathetic, full of quaint imaginings and irrelevant relevancies, a style to which something is owed by almost every subsequent writer of such essays as are primarily works of art.

Prose-Poetry

60. There is De Quincey's prose-poetry, the parent of Ruskin's purple patch and some sort of a relation to Pater's and Wilde's and Galsworthy's aesthetic styles. It aimed deliberately at introducing into prose the imagination and the magniloquence at that time generally associated only with verse, so that De Quincey thought he had invented a new prose when he wrote :

> Vain prayer! Empty adjuration! Profitless rebellion against the laws which season all things for the inexorable grave! Yet not the less we rebel again and again; and, though wisdom counsels resignation, yet our human passions, still cleaving to their object, force us into endless rebellion.... Phantoms of lost power, sudden intuitions, and shadowy restorations of forgotten feelings — sometimes dim and perplexing, sometimes by bright but furtive glimpses, sometimes by a full and steady revelation, overcharged with light — throw us back in a moment upon scenes and remembrances that we have left full thirty years behind us.

True Classical Style

61. There is Landor's style, which aims at the simplicity and finish, the restraint and leisure of Greek art, but avoids the narrowness and artificiality of the eighteenth century pseudo-classic :

> Ionia is far more beautiful than Attica, Miletus than Athens; for about Athens there is no verdure, no spacious and full and flowing river, few gardens, many olive-trees, so many indeed that we seem to be in an eternal cloud of dust. However, when the sea-breezes blow, this tree itself looks beautiful; it looks, in its pliable and undulating branches, irresolute as Ariadne when she was urged to fly, and pale as Orithyia when she was borne away.

Carlylese

62. As complete a contrast to this as can be found is Carlyle's style, grotesque, disjointed, vivid, full of queer compounds and queer words, odd inversions and odder omissions of the less important parts of speech, a style perhaps over-loud, over-emphatic, but thoroughly alive :

> Johnson's youth was poor, isolated, hopeless, very miserable.... The largest soul that was in all England; and provision made for it of "fourpence-halfpenny a day."...Rude, stubborn self-help here; a whole world of squalor, rudeness, confused misery and want, yet of nobleness and manfulness withal.... Very curious how, in that poor Paper-age, so barren, artificial, thick-quilted with Pedantries, Hearsays, the great Fact of this Universe glared in, forever wonderful, indubitable, unspeakable, divine-infernal, upon this man too!

Dickensian Style

63. Somewhat akin to Carlyle's style in mastery of the grotesque and in force is Dickens's; but in Dickens's prose there is nothing of the merely eccentric. He gets his effects mainly by an eye for detail, by a vivid interest in everything and everybody, by an imagination which sees odd resemblances — an imagination, indeed, something like that of the best Metaphysicals — by an almost unparalleled sense of humour and by a gift of exuberant description. Consequently, whereas Carlyle's influence on style has been almost wholly bad — even Meredith learnt as many faults as virtues from him — Dickens has formed a good model for hundreds of beginners and has taught much to many, such as Chesterton, who are not beginners.

Romantic Movement in Verse

64. Meanwhile a very similar development had been taking place in verse. The Romantic movement began even before the death of Pope; in fact, it is truer to say that the Romantic element never completely died out of English literature, though — under Dryden and Pope — it was temporarily eclipsed. But towards the end of the century the new movement gained force and took on a more clearly defined manner.

The New Simplicity

65. As the simple prose of Addison had given place to the pomp of Johnson, so the clear, plain verse of Dryden had given place to the rather stilted "poetic diction" of Gray and of the lesser followers of Milton. But whereas prose writers as a whole made no attempt to return to simplicity, the verse writers, however much they differed in other ways, agreed in a preference for the natural. Burns wrote songs which regain the ease and clearness of Herrick but avoid his courtly artificiality of sentiment; Blake, with the melody and freshness of the Elizabethans, adds an almost childlike note — a suggestion even of the nursery, rime; Crabbe describes with painstaking fidelity the sordid realities of life; Wordsworth aims at writing the language of common men. The similarity between these four in this matter is evident :

> I see her in the dewy flowers,
>   I see her sweet and fair :
> I hear her in the tunefu' birds,
>   I hear her charm the air.

> To this day they dwell
> In a lonely dell,
> Nor fear the wolvish how!
> Nor the lion's growl.

Some few in town observed in Peter's trap
A boy, with jacket blue and woollen cap;
But none enquired how Peter used the rope,
Or what the bruise, that made the stripling stoop,
None could the ridges on his back behold,
None sought him shiv'ring in the winter's cold.

Even yet thou art to me
No bird; but an invisible thing,
A voice, a mystery.

But this is not the simplicity we have already met; it is neither the simplicity of the unpractised hand nor the highly finished structural simplicity of a Tennyson or a Dickens; it is something between the two — a more or less deliberate discarding of the trappings of verse, an effort to use simple words as well as simple sentences, and to deal with primitive ideas and impressions. The method has its dangers; Burns avoids them, but Blake is sometimes babyish, Crabbe is often dull and ugly, Wordsworth can begin what he thinks an eerie tale with :

Oh! what's the matter ? what's the matter?
What is't that ails young Harry Gill?
That evermore his teeth they chatter,
Chatter, chatter, chatter still!
Of waistcoats Harry has no lack,
Good duffle grey, and flannel fine;
He has a blanket on his back,
And coats enough to smother nine.

a series of commonplaces — chattering teeth, flannel waistcoats, blankets and coats — which provokes a smile.

Indeed, a severely plain style is too narrow even for prose; for poetry it is still more unsuited. The protest, partly conscious, partly unconscious, against the stagey black-velvet-and-tinsel diction of Gray's imitators was necessary; but, when once it had been made effectively, poetry discovered a new, a more natural magnificence.

The New Exuberance

Comic Verse

66. Keats brought back the Spenserian pictorial power and, in *Hyperion,* the stately march of Milton; Byron, in his most characteristic work, gave us what is still our best comic verse :

> And therefore will I leave off metaphysical
> Discussion, which is neither here nor there :
> If I agree that what is, is : then this I call
> Being quite perspicuous and extremely fair.
> The truth is, I've grown lately rather phthisical :
> I don't know what the reason is — the air,
> Perhaps; but, as I suffer from the shocks
> Of illness, I grow much more orthodox.

where we find quaint rimes *(metaphysical...this I call...phthisical; shocks...orthodox);* a frivolity of sentiment well-matched with frivolity of speech; careless *colloquialisms — neither here nor there, ... , the truth is...I don't know;* and, in the whole poem, and occasionally in a single stanza, abrupt changes from grave to gay, from apparently sincere feeling to a mocking cynicism which denies the existence of any feelings except greed and hatred.

The Insubstantial Style

67. Shelley's style is as abstract and etherial as Byron's is concrete and worldly. He does not give you Keats's mediaeval miniatures, crowded with detail in bright clear colours; he gives you dim, vague, fairy landscapes bathed in opalescent moonlight. If he writes of a sky-lark, he will compare it to a "poet, hidden in the night of thought," on the well-known educational principle of explaining the familiar by the unfamiliar; he will write you a drama in which figure not only earth but the spirit of earth as well; he will fill you a stanza with abstract ideas :

> And like a storm bursting its cloudy prison
> With thunder, and with whirlwind, has arisen
> Out of the lampless caves of unimagined being :

With earthquake shock and swiftness making shiver
Thought's stagnant chaos, unremoved for ever,
Till hate, and fear, and pain, light-vanquished shadows,
fleeing
Leave man, who was a many-sided mirror.

68. That *has* a "meaning," in the common man's sense of the word — a meaning which can be expressed in plain prose or translated into another tongue — but it is not this "meaning" that gives the poetry, its value; it is, we fear, possible for some lovers of Shelley to read it without catching sight of this "meaning" at all. For the true meaning of poetry, is not a constant quantity — its real significance is whatever it means to the reader, all the pictures and ideas, thoughts and dreams, feelings and phantoms which it sets hovering round his head.

69. Judged by this standard, the Augustan school takes a very low place; judged by this standard Shelley's poetry ranks with the very greatest in the language — higher even than the bulk of Keats and Tennyson. If you doubt this, apply your "list" test. Saying ten characteristic lines of Shelley, Pope, Keats, and Tennyson over and over to yourself, write down all the ideas which suggest themselves, then compare your four lists. It is safe to say that the Pope list will contain mainly reasonings; in the Keats and Tennyson lists beautiful pictures will predominate; while the Shelley list will be longer, containing besides pictures more unusual and more varied and emotions more intense and more lofty, both reasonings and the less logical and less closely knit kinds of thought.

70. On succeeding poets Shelley has had a great influence. His use of the abstract to illustrate the concrete, his fondness for lofty rhetoric packed full of thought, as in :

To suffer woes which Hope thinks infinite;

his fairy-like scenery, all helped to mould writers utterly different from him in thought and outlook.

The first two of these characteristics — often, alas! without the rich beauty of melody and image — are found in Matthew

Arnold, who thought Shelley ineffectual — though Arnold owes much here to Wordsworth, too — and in Hardy, whose philosophy of life is diametrically opposed to Shelley's; his fairy note is re-echoed by Beddoes and, with a purely individual touch of grotesque elfin humour, by Walter de la Mare; his swift melody by Tennyson and Swinburne.

The New Realism

71. Shelley's influence on Tennyson, however, though not slight, was nothing like go strong as that of Keats. Tennyson indeed has many styles, only one of which perhaps is sufficiently new and sufficiently important to mention here. This is the new scientific-detailed style. The old poets who used detail would describe things familiar to all — rooks flying home at sunset, pink-tipped daisies studding the meadow, the dewdrops hanging on the morning grass : Tennyson used unfamiliar detail — he studied Nature with the scientist's exactitude,

> More black than ash-buds in the front of March

he will say; and we go out into the garden to discover with surprise that ash-buds in March *are* black.

Romantic Realism

72. This new realism has developed much since Tennyson's day. It is no longer a mere realism in the description of beautiful natural objects; it has incorporated the sordid realism of Crabbe, but it has not left it merely sordid — it makes it vivid, secret, exciting, even beautiful. There is nothing beautiful about Quilp in real life, but Dickens's Quilp gives us the same romantic thrill as Scott's Ivanhoe.

73. Browning is the first poet of importance to adopt this style. No one could call *The Pied Piper of Hamelin* merely ugly, merely grotesque, merely romantic. It has a queer individual beauty, and it is as full of realism as of improbability. Browning, like Swift before him, though without Swift's "classical" imperturbability, writes of the impossible as if it were matter-of-fact; you have only to think what the story would have become in Poe's hands or Maeterlinck's or Walter de la Mare's to grasp the difference between romantic realism and pure romanticism.

The Shorthand Style

74. Browning's realism is many-sided, not a mere choice of realistic detail. It is above all realism in the expression of thought. Browning, except where his learning leads him to make obscure allusions, is not difficult to understand when once you have the key to his strangeness. We all write as we think English should be written or, if we have not reached those heights, as we speak : Browning writes as he thinks. There is a vast gulf between the two : our mental processes are not entirely logical, not entirely complete, certainly not rounded into syntactical perfection. We get a half-glimpse of an idea and then, before we have time to examine it thoroughly, it changes with kaleidoscopic rapidity into something else. Nor are our thoughts bare intellectual things; they are obscurely tinged with feelings, prejudices, instincts, of which we ourselves are often only half-conscious. Browning made it his business first of all to become more fully conscious of the contents of his own or his characters' mind, and then to express his new knowledge in the abrupt, colloquial style natural to those who are thinking aloud. Browning's Bishop Blougram, for instance, speaks in this way of the voyage of life :

> You peep up from your utterly naked boards
> Into some snug and well-appointed berth,
> Like mine, for instance (try the cooler jug —
> Put back the other, but don't jog the ice)
> And mortified you mutter "Well and good —
> He sits enjoying his sea-furniture —
> 'Tis stout and proper, and there's store of it,
> Though I've the better notion, all agree,
> Of fitting rooms up!"

Our acquaintance with bishops may not be sufficient for us to determine whether this is how they talk; but — except for an imaginative knack of metaphor not too common — it is very much how ordinary folk talk, breaking off their argument to offer refreshment, going on again unperturbed with colloquial turns of speech, with a little sarcastic half-smile at "mine, for instance," with a broader smile — to take out the sting — as he half-accuses his guest of "swank."

To make such a passage intelligible to the bearer what is necessary above all is to get the expression right, to emphasise this word, throw a half-laugh into that hint, a question in a third — to read it with the very tone and gesture of natural and unrestrained speech.

Browning did not take the process to its logical conclusion; his work is necessarily a compromise, but it is a compromise much nearer to "standard" English than the work of Meredith or of Henry James. These analyse more minutely, record more exactly, hedge, qualify their statements, explain with conscientious particularity what their heroine thought at 5.56 and what she was beginning to think at 5.57; they reproduce faithfully the half-sentences, the hints and shrugs of talk between quick-witted and sensitive modern people. Consider this passage from Meredith's *One of Our Conquerors* :

> She begged a day's delay; which would enable her, she said, to join them in dining at the Blachington's, and seeing dear Lake-lands again. "I was invited, you know." She spoke in childish style, and under her eyes she beheld her father and mother exchange looks. He had a fear that Nataly might support the girl's petition. Nataly read him to mean possible dangers among the people at Wrensham. She had seemed hesitating. After meeting Victor's look, her negative was firm. She tried to make it one of distress for the use of the negative to her own dear girl. Nesta spied beneath.

That gives us the essence of a fairly long conversation between three people; yet only two speak, and of these one says only "No." The rest of the conversation consists of looks and thoughts.

This, then, is the new cryptic style, an application to thought and speech of the new realism hitherto kept for concrete externalities. Side by side with it, the realism of description continues, borrowing some of its neighbour's economy of words. The verbless sentence, already not uncommon in Dickens, becomes frequent. Sinclair Lewis can write :

> Under the rolling clouds of prairie a moving mass of steel. An irritable clank and rattle beneath a prolonged roar. The sharp scent of oranges cutting the soggy smell of unbathed people and ancient baggage.
>
> Towns are planless as a scattering of pasteboard boxes on an attic floor. The stretch of faded gold stubble broken only by clumps of willows encircling white houses and red barns.

Bart Kennedy and a crowd of minor impressionistic writers can go even further than this in the simplification of language, and write a prose almost entirely composed of disconnected nouns and adjectives with a few infinitive parts of verbs.

Futurist Style

75. Still bolder, the futurist writer disintegrates the language completely, using mathematical and musical signs, dispensing with stops, inventing onomatopoeic words, writing, say, to represent a child falling and being comforted :

> Father and child (tb-tb tb-tb) plomp plomp kersquosh boo-hoo > hoo ps ps boo > smile.

Free Verse

76. This, he may tell us, is poetry. But where, you may ask, is the metre? He will tell you that metre is a fetter, a convention, with which he has nothing to do. Long before the ultra-modernist invented a language of his own, the revolt against metrical form had begun — a revolt headed by the great American poet, Walt Whitman. But these writers of free verse did not despise rhythm itself; what they wrote was a highly rhythmical, cadenced prose, generally though not always arranged in verse lines to match the cadences.

Though some of us may prefer regular verse or a less mannered prose, we cannot today honestly deny the beauty of much of this work. So it is possible that our grandchildren may find beauty even in Futurism, just as our ancestors found beauty in woad-stencilled faces.

77. The realistic school, then, appears to have gone, in its jazz discords, as far as it is possible for it to go. But it has not killed the aesthetic school. It is a feature of the last century that, alongside the attempt to reproduce with fidelity its ugliness and grotesqueness there was always, in strong contrast, an attempt to reduce all life to sheer beauty. As Browning was the head and fount of modern realism, so Tennyson was the father of modern aestheticism, the aestheticism which does not, as did Keats, exclude "unpoetical" subjects, which does not necessarily (as did Keats) ignore "moral purpose" in the interests of art, but which consciously or unconsciously places art first.

Pre-Raphaelite Style

78. Some of the Pre-Raphaelite group, indeed, were immensely interested in politics and in economics — William Morris was even a capable business-man — but their first aim was to bring back to English style the intricate detail, the simplicity of drawing and colouring characteristic of painting before Raphael. Morris himself had a peculiar fondness for the Anglo-Saxon element in the English language; he resuscitated many dead words, coined others, and with much ingenuity succeeded in writing pages of prose quite free from Latin-derived words. At its best his prose and verse are like a clear, gently-flowing stream in green English fields; at its worst they have something of the insipidity and monotony of a trickle from the tap.

79. His friend D.G. Rossetti depended for his effect mainly upon richness of detail and of colouring; he is the Burne Jones of literature, indeed many of his poems are little more than descriptions of a picture or related series of pictures. Thus two or three pictures — or two or three stained glass windows — could give us almost the whole content of "The Blessèd Damozel" : we should see her first standing at the gold bar of Heaven eagerly looking down for her lover; a second picture would show her again, with the gathering shadow of weary disappointment on her face; the third would show her, head dropped on hands, in tears; round the borders miniatures would give the substance of the stanzas in which she imagines herself wandering with him.

80. If Rossetti is the painter and sculptor in verse, Swinburne is the musician. His use of alliteration (see page 14) is only the most obvious element in a complex harmony, a swift rush and clangour of wonderful sound. Swinburne has had an enormous influence over the eager, passionate section of modern aesthetes, Fitzgerald over the languid, fatalistic section.

Symbolistic Style

81. In prose, Ruskin, Pater, Stevenson, Wilde among the elder men, Galsworthy and Masefield among the younger, are perhaps the most prominent. But if, especially in the later of these writers, realism is made to serve the purposes of aestheticism, in Yeats and several others of the Irish school unreality is put to the same use. We have strange, dim, remote figures from another world; unfamiliar birds, shadowy trees — and all these are vague symbols of ideas, spiritual realities which lie beyond and behind them. The weirdness is increased by the contrast with an occasional Irish — and therefore to English readers not entirely real — realism, and by the use of an Irish mythology still not very familiar to English readers. Take, for instance, the following from *The Player Queen* :

> Leave me to die alone? I do not blame you. There is courage in red wine, in white wine, in beer, even in thin beer sold by a blear-eyed potboy in a bankrupt tavern, but there is none in the human heart. When my master the Unicorn bathes by the light of the Great

> Bear, and to the sound of Tabors, even the sweet river-water makes him drunk; but it is cold, it is cold, alas! it is cold.

Here we begin with a statement as intelligible as need be — that all courage is "Dutch courage" — expressed in a limpid, rhythmical prose which makes even the blear-eyed potboy beautiful. But, passing from the realism of the bankrupt tavern, we seem to step into another world — a fairy world in which mystic Unicorns bathe to the sound of tabors. The swiftness of the transition, the strangeness of the contrast fill the reader with a sense of the uncanny, of another world; secret and beautiful, remote from ours and yet close around it — or, if he be a scoffer, with a wild laughter.

For it is not merely the mad, the sick, and the drunken who speak so; this is the common speech of common men. It is the method of *Alice in Wonderland* refined, etherialised, and applied to serious purposes.

New Intellectualism

Style of Epigrammatic Levity

82. Alongside the new aestheticism — and, indeed, often combined with it — we find a new intellectualism, a kind of cross between the wit of the old Restoration Comedy and of Sheridan, and the attempts of Arnold, both in prose and verse, to think systematically, to make a cultured reason the final arbiter in all human problems. This new interest in the things of the mind takes many forms; in Wilde it is brilliant, superficial, epigrammatic :

> "The ancient historians gave us delightful fiction in the form of fact; the modern novelist presents us with dull facts under the guise of fiction.... Many a young man starts in life with a natural gift for exaggeration which, if nurtured in congenial and sympathetic surroundings, or by the imitation of the best models, might grow into something really great and wonderful.

> But, as a rule, he comes to nothing. He either falls into careless habits of accuracy —"
>
> CYRIL. My dear fellow!
>
> VIVIAN. Please don't interrupt in the middle of a sentence. "He either falls into careless habits of accuracy, or takes to frequenting the society of the aged and the well-informed.... I quite admit that modern novels have many good points. All I insist on is that, as a class, they are quite unreadable."

Here the effort to be clever is as evident as the effort to write beautifully. The frequent, but not too frequent, antithesis; the air of nonchalant matter-of-fact with which such well-worn phrases as 'careless habits of inaccuracy" are given an entirely unexpected turn; the way in which the dialogue-form is used to emphasise the writer's wit — lest a reader who has not yet fallen into careless habits of accuracy should miss the point —Vivian's own deliberate artistry, which cannot endure an interruption of the rhythmic flow of his artfully balanced sentence —all these are marks of the intellectual-aesthetic style.

83. Now let us turn to Shaw's Preface to *Androcles and the Lion* :

> It seems therefore that we must begin by holding the right to an income as sacred and equal, just as we now begin by holding the right to life as sacred and equal. Indeed, the one right is only a restatement of the other. To hang me for cutting a dock labourer's throat after making much of me for leaving him to starve when I do not happen to have a ship for him to unload is idiotic; for as he does far less mischief with his throat cut than when he is starving, a rational society would esteem the cut-throat more highly than the capitalist.

or, for his dialogue style, to his *Man and Superman* :

> OCTAVIUS. I believe most intensely in the dignity of labour.

STRAKER (*unimpressed*). That's because you never done any, Mr. Robinson. My business is to do away with labour. You'll get more out of me and a machine than you will out of twenty labourers, and not so much to drink either.

The style in both cases is hard, bright, clever, appearing at times to cover as earnest purpose with a cloak of buffoonery. There is nothing of Wilde's semi-poetic phrases, there is no attempt at "fine writing"; this prose is clear, nervous, entirely devoid of conventional literary turns, full of illustrations drawn from the plain man's experience, full of statements which strike one at first sight as — to use his own colloquial phrase — "idiotic," but which prove on closer examination to enshrine a serious idea.

In many ways, then, Shaw recalls Swift — but a sharperwitted Swift with less depth of emotion. Note, too, his realistic representation of modern uncultured speech — its neglect of syntax and its downright conciseness and clarity. Chesterton's prose, another example of the new intellectualism, we have already considered.

84. But perhaps the most striking illustration of the extent to which reason sways the modern writer is to be found, not in drama and not in the essay, but in the novel. By their very form the play and the essay adapt themselves to the development of a thesis, but the novel from its beginning was essentially a story told for amusement, not instruction. Throughout its history it had been a loose mould into which the author could pour characterisation, episode, descriptive writing, philosophising — anything, in short, which occurred to him, provided only that what he wrote was interesting. But in these last days has appeared the novel with an idea — the problem novel, as it is sometimes inaccurately called. Galsworthy will write a trilogy — with a few shorter afterthoughts — on the development in the last century of the Man of Property type, the acquisitive Englishman, almost completely materialist in practice if not in theory, anxious only to "get on" and to possess; Wells will write novel after novel to illustrate the need of a wiser education, a more carefully trained race. More and more the novelist gets his material not from life but from that cubist reflection of life — the psychological treatise; novelist after novelist will attack the abuses of the time — the growth of trusts, Press monopolies, patent-medicine fortunes, and so on — making their attack not, as Dickens did, a part, however large a part, of a novel, but constructing the whole of his novel round the one central idea.

As a natural consequence, the style of the novel is profoundly modified : the old "once-upon-a-time" narrative manner has largely disappeared. Contrast, for instance, with the first lines of a novel by Dickens or Thackeray or of a modern "yarn-teller" like De Morgan or Conrad the opening of Wells's *The Research Magnificent* :

THE PRELUDE
On Fear and Aristocracy

Explanatory-Narrative Style

> The story of William Porphyry Benham is the story of a man who was led into adventure by an idea. It was an idea that took possession of his imagination quite early in life, it grew with him and changed with him, it interwove at last completely with his being,

and so on for some pages. Could anything be less suggestive of an interest in the story as a story? This new style is above all explanatory : it is concerned to make you understand the writer's purpose and point of view; it is carefully and deliberately reasonable.

Cynical Sentimentalism

85. Perhaps the extreme example of the way in which the modern has become self-conscious is to be found in J.M. Barrie. To many a casual reader he is an amusing sentimentalist or a "dear man, so funny and so pathetic" — nothing more. But very little consideration is enough to convince us that Barrie is by no means a mere sentimentalist : he is possessed of an ironic insight as clear as Hardy's : he has learnt the lesson of Ibsen's *Wild Duck* that even harmful illusions may be better for the weak than no illusions at all. If we only realised it, he says in effect, most of our emotions are factitious and theatrical; Mr. Darling will take delight in parading his repentance long after he has ceased to be sorry; Sentimental Tommy will bear himself as a hero suffering agonies when he has merely *imagined* that his ankle is injured; when Mary Rose comes back to her heart-broken father, he wishes she had stayed away; your journalist will make of his deepest agonies material for humorous copy — only mother-love is retal — and yet Peter Pan's mother shuts him out when she gets another child. Barrie's style matches his thought — he is perhaps of all our modern writers the most consciously artistic, the most capable of getting from a single phrase or even a single word a whole complicated world of thought-shot emotion. There are traces of this even in his early novel *Better Dead* :

> Andrew is now a staunch Conservative. Domesticated and repentant, he has renounced the devil and all her works. Sometimes, when thinking of the past, the babble of his lovely babies jars upon him, and, still half-dreaming, he brings their heads close together.
>
> At such a time all the anxious mother has to say is —
>
> "Andrew !"
>
> Then with a start he lays them gently in a heap on the floor, and, striding the room, soon regains his composure.

Note here the sly humour in the devil's change of sex, the gentle under-statement in "knocks their heads together" — "drops them" would entirely spoil the passage — the half-mockery of the semi-poetical alliteration in "babble of his lovely babies."

86. And — perhaps as one more unconscious expression of the universal desire for contrast — we get, alongside this self-conscious, extremely sophisticated prose, the childlike songs of such modern lyrists as Ralph Hodgson — songs whose style has affinities both with the Elizabethans and with Blake.

In our time, indeed, something of the great variety of style evident in the Elizabethan period is again apparent : whether our new heterogeneity will be followed by the narrowness of a new classicism remains to be seen.

Journalese

87. But if, among, the many highly individual styles in our highly individual literature, lack of space has compelled the neglect of many great names, there is one style, associated with no great name, which cannot be overlooked, so characteristic of our age is it — the Journalistic style. It has its origin in the conditions of the modern press, conditions which oblige hundreds of people to write at great speed in an arresting manner of matters of which they are more or less ignorant. The more skilful and better educated of these hundreds often produce a style which differs from good plain English prose mainly in a heightening of the contrasts of light and shade, an avoidance of all "heavy" reading, and a stressing of the "human element"; the less skilful try to make up by a pontifical manner, and a bastard Johnsonese for their consciousness of ignorance, to save time and thought by the use of outworn phrases, and to arrest and startle by crude, over-coloured descriptions. If they lack proper training, they add grammatical blunders to their other faults. So we may get would-be fine writing of this kind :

> The approaching festival at the Little Applingdon Village Hall will, we can assure our readers with the greatest confidence, surpass all expectations. Constable Smith, our feared and revered man in blue, will be there, arrayed in official panoply, and will give a recitation from one of the deathless works of the immortal Swan of Avon; Miss Smith, who will wear a wonderful creation in *soie de choux* and *crêpe-de-chine,* and which will rouse the envy of all beholders, will give a vocal performance of the first water; and the Reverend Paisley, full of the milk of human kindness, will again bless our proceedings with his fatherly smile.

EXERCISE III

1. Attempt a classification of the following passages as (*a*) ornate, (*b*) simple.

2. Which of the following extracts do you consider appeal primarily to (*a*) your feelings, (*b*) your sense of beauty, (*c*) your sense of humour, (*d*) your mind? Give reasons for your opinion.

3. Consider each of the following extracts and say to which variety or varieties of style mentioned in Chapter 3 you assign it. Give your reasons. If you think it represents a variety not mentioned there, describe its style.

4. Arrange the following extracts in what you consider their approximate chronological order.

1. It was his luxurious custom to shave while sitting snugly in a tubful of hot water. He may be viewed to-night as a plump, smooth, pink, baldish, podgy goodman, robbed of the importance of spectacles, squatting in breast-high water, scraping his lather-smeared cheeks with a safety-razor like a tiny lawn-mower, and with melancholy dignity clawing through the water to recover a slippery and active piece of soap.

2. A sea-bird, cackling like a devil, spoke
And the fog, drew away and hung like lead :
Like mighty cliffs it shaped, sullen and red,
Like glowering gods at watch it did appear,
And sometimes drew away and then drew near.

Like islands and like chasms and like hell,
But always mighty and red, gloomy and ruddy,
Shutting the visible sea in like a wall,
Slow-heaving in vast ripples blank and muddy
Where the sun should have risen it streaked bloody.

3. Spatter. Whirr! Whirr!
"Toward that patch of brown;
Direction left." Bullets a stream
Devouring thought crying in a dream.
Men, crumpled, going down....

Go on. Go.
Deafness, Numbness, The loudening tornado.
Bullets. Mud. Stumbling and skating.
My voice's strangled shout :
"Steady pace, boys!"

4. Babel Tower, with the confusion of tongues, were not Bedlam added with the conflagration of thoughts, was no type of it. One forest of distracted steel bristles, endless, in front of an Electoral Committee; points itself, in horrid radii, against this and the other accused breast. It was the Titans warring with Olympus; and they, scarcely crediting it, have *conquered* : prodigy of prodigies; delirious, — as it could not but be. Denunciation, vengeance, blaze of triumph on a dark ground of terror; all outward, all inward things fallen into one general wreck of madness!

5. Cranes and gaudy parrots go
Up and down the burning sky;
Tree-top cats purr drowsily
In the dim-day green below;
And troops of monkeys, nutting, some,
All disputing, go and come;
And things abominable sit
Picking offal buck or swine,
On the mesh and over it
Burnished flies and beetles shine,
And spiders big as bladders lie
Under hemlocks ten foot high.

6. A paradoxical writer like Bernard 8haw is perpetually and tiresomely told that he stands on his head. But all romance and all religion consist in making the whole universe stand on its head. That reversal is the whole idea of virtue; that the last shall be first and the first last.

7. Jack was quite as much a part of the village as the church spire;

And if any of us lazied along by the river in the dusk of the evening —

Waving aside nebulae of gnats,
Turning head quickly at the splash of a jumping fish,
Peering where the water chuckled over a vanishing water-rat —
And saw not Jack's familiar form bending over his lines,
And smelt not his vile shag,
We should feel a loneliness, a vague impression that something was wrong.

8. In fact, a sense of something whimsical in their companionship seems to have taken entire possession of his rude brain. The bare fact of being patronised by a great man whom he could have crushed with one hand, appeared in his eyes so eccentric and humorous, that a kind of ferocious merriment gained the mastery over him, and quite subdued his brutal nature. He roared and roared again; toasted Mr. Tappertit a hundred times; declared himself a Bull-dog to the core; and vowed to be faithful to him to the last drop of blood in his veins.

9. Beneath me in the valley waves the palm.
Beneath, beyond the valley, breaks the sea;
Beneath me sleep in mist and light and calm
Cities of Lebanon, dream-shadow-dim,
Where Kings of Tyre and Kings of Tyre did rule
In ancient days in endless dynasty,
And all around the snowy mountains swim
Like mighty swans afloat in heaven's pool.

10. Darkness had gathered; the moon was rising; over the door the reflections of those old boar-spears branched sharp and long on the pale wall; they had an uncanny look, like cross-bones. How those two fellows disliked each other! Whole centuries of antagonism glared out of their eyes. They seemed to sum up in some mysterious way all that's significant and opposed in the artist and the man of action.... One represented a decent well-fed spirit of satisfaction with things as they are, and the other a ravening shade, whom centuries of starvation had engrained with strife.

11. Barbary and her husband away before us. We stayed till, it being darkish, we saw the fire as only one entire arch of fire from this to the other side the bridge, and in a bow up the hill for an arch of above a mile long : it made me weep to see it. The churches, houses, and all on fire, and flaming at once; and a horrid noise the flames made, and the cracking of houses at their ruin.

So home with a sad heart, and there find everybody discoursing and lamenting the fire; and poor Tom Hater came with some few of his goods saved out of his house, which was burned upon Fish Street Hill.

12. They rush in red and purple from the red clouds of the morn,
From temples where the yellow gods shut up their eyes in scorn;
They rise in green robes roaring from the green hells of the sea
Where fallen skies and evil hues and eyeless creatures be;
On them the sea-valves cluster and the grey sea-forests curl,
Splashed with a splendid sickness, the sickness of the pearl;
They swell in sapphire smoke out of the blue cracks of the ground, —
They gather and they wonder and give worship to Mahound.

13. And the wandering of many roads hath made my eyes
As dark red circles filled with dust.
Yet there is a trembling upon me in the twilight,
And little red elf words crying "A song,"
Little grey elf words crying for a song,
Little brown leaf words crying "A song,"
Little green leaf words crying for a song.

The words are as leaves, old brown leaves in the spring
time
Blowing they know not whither, seeking a song.

14. I saw then in my dream, so far as this valley reached, there was on the right hand a very deep ditch; that ditch is it into which the blind have led the blind in all ages, and have both there miserably perished. Again, behold on the left hand there was a very dangerous quag, in which if even a good man falls he finds no bottom for his foot to stand on. Into that quag King David once did fall, and had no doubt therein been smothered, had not he that is able plucked him out.

15. The style of Dryden is capricious and varied; that of Pope is cautious and uniform. Dryden observes the motions of his own mind; Pope constrains his mind to his own rules of composition. Dryden is sometimes vehement and rapid; Pope is always smooth, uniform, and gentle. Dryden's page is a natural field, rising into inequalities, and diversified by the varied exuberance of abundant vegetation; Pope's is a velvet lawn, shaven by the scythe, and levelled by the roller.

16. He could distinguish, and divide
A hair 'twixt south and south-west side;
On either which he would dispute,
Confute, change hands, and still confute :
He'd undertake to prove, by force
Of argument, a man's no horse;
He'd prove a buzzard is no fowl,
And that a lord may be an owl,
A calf an alderman, a goose a justice,
And rooks committee men and trustees.
He'd run in debt by disputation,
And pay with ratiocination.

17. The crystal springs whose taste illuminates
Refinéd eyes with an eternal sight,
Like triéd silver run through Paradise
To entertain divine Zenocrate :
The cherubims and holy seraphins,

That sing and play before the King of Kings
Use all their voices and their instruments
To entertain divine Zenocrate;
And, in this sweet and curious harmony,
The god that tunes this music to our souls
Holds out his hand in highest majesty
To entertain divine Zonocrate.

18. Air shudders with shrill spears crossing, and hurtling of wheels that roar.
As the grinding of teeth in the jaws of a lion that foam as they gnash
Is the shriek of the axles that loosen, the shook of the poles that crash.
The dense manes darken and glitter, the mouths of the mad steeds champ,
Their heads flash blind through the battle, and death's foot rings in their tramp.

19. Sad is the day, and worse must follow, when we hear the blackbird in the garden, and do not throb with joy. But, Leofric, the high festival is strown by the servant of God upon the heart of man. It is gladness, it is thanksgiving; it is the orphan, the starveling, pressed to the bosom, and bidden as its first commandment to remember its benefactor. We will hold this festival; the guests are ready; we may keep it up for weeks, and months, and years together, and always be the happier and the richer for it. The beverage of this feast, O Leofric, is sweeter than bee or flower or vine can give us : it flows from heaven; and in heaven will it abundantly be poured out again to him who pours it out here abundantly.

20. My lords, if you must fall, may you so fall! But if you stand, and stand I trust you will, together with the fortune of this ancient monarchy — together with the ancient laws and liberties of this great and illustrious kingdom — may you stand as unimpeached in honour as in power; may you stand not as a substitute for virtue, but as an ornament of virtue, as a security for virtue; may you stand long, and long stand the terror of tyrants; may you stand the refuge of afflicted nations; may you stand a sacred temple, for the perpetual residence of an inviolable justice.

21. The eldest of the three is named *Mater Lachrymarum,* Our Lady of Tears. She it is that night and day raves and moans, calling for vanished faces. She stood in Rama, where a voice was heard of lamentation, — Rachel weeping for her children, and refusing to be comforted. She it was that stood in Bethlehem on the night when Herod's sword swept its nurseries of innocents, and the little feet were stiffened for ever, which, heard at times as they tottered along floors overhead, woke pulses of love in household hearts that were not unmarked in heaven. Her eyes are sweet and subtle, wild and sleepy, by turns; oftentimes rising to the clouds, oftentimes challenging the heavens. She wears a diadem round her head. And I knew by childish memories that she could go abroad upon the winds, when she heard the sobbing of litanies or the thundering of organs, and when she beheld the mustering of summer clouds.

22. Envy the next, Envy with squinted eyes;
Sick of a strange disease, his neighbour's health;
Best lives he then when any better dies,
Is never poor but in another's wealth.
On best men's harms and griefs he feeds his fill,
Else his own maw doth eat with spiteful will.
Ill must the temper be, where diet is so ill.

23. A fiery soul, which, working out its way,
Fretted the pigmy body to decay,
And o'er-informed the tenement of clay.
A daring pilot in extremity,
Pleased with the danger, when the waves went high
He sought the storms; but for a calm unfit,
Would steer too nigh the sands, to boast his wit.
Great wits are sure to madness near allied,
And thin partitions do their bounds divide.
Else why should he, with wealth and honour blest,

Refuse his age the needful hours of rest?
Punish a body which he could not please;
Bankrupt of life, yet prodigal of ease?

24. And as Night's chariot through the air was driven,
Clamour grew dumb, unheard was shepherd's song,
And silence girt the woods; no warbling tongue
Talked to the echo; satyrs broke their dance,
And all the upper world lay in a trance.
Only the curled streams soft chidings kept,
And little gales that from the green leaf swept
Dry summer's dust, in fearful whisperings stirred
As loath to waken any singing bird.

25. We could never quite understand the philosophy of this arrangement, or the wisdom of our ancestors in sending us for instruction to those woolly bedfellows. A sheep, when it is dark, has nothing to do but to shut his silly eyes, and sleep if he can. Man found out long sixes.— Hail candlelight! without disparagement to sun or moon, the kindliest luminary of the three — if we may not rather style thee their radiant deputy, mild viceroy of the moon! We love to read, talk, sit silent, eat, drink, sleep, by candle-light. They are everybody's sun and moon. This is our peculiar and household planet.

26. The consternation of Gaul was universal; and the various fortunes of its cities have been adorned by tradition with martyrdoms and miracles. Troyes was saved by the merits of St. Lupus; St. Servatius was removed from the world, that he might not behold the ruin of Tongres; and the prayers of St. Genevieve diverted the march of Attila from the neighbourhood of Paris. But as the greatest part of the Gallic cities were alike destitute of saints and soldiers, they were besieged and stormed by the Huns; who practised, in the example of Metz, their customary maxims of war.

27. To Israel

Honour hath left and freedom, let but them
Find courage to lay hold on this occasion;
To himself and father's house eternal fame;

And, which is best and happiest yet, all this
With God not parted from him, as was feared,
But favouring and assisting to the end.
Nothing is here for tears, nothing to wail,
Or knock the breast; no weakness, no contempt,
Dispraise, or blame; nothing but well and fair,
And what may quiet us in a death so noble

28. Does he really think of making us enamoured of the "good old times" by the faithful and harrowing portraits he has drawn of them? Would he carry us back to the early stages of barbarism, of clanship, of the feudal system, as a "consummation devoutly to be wished"? Is he infatuated enough, or does he so doat and drivel over his own slothful and self-willed prejudices, as to believe that he will make a single convert to the beauty of Legitimacy, that is, of lawless power and savage bigotry, when he himself is obliged to apologise for the horrors he describes, and even render his descriptions credible to the modern reader by referring to the authentic history of these delectable times?

29. Next him was Feare, all arm'd from top to toe,
Yet thought himselfe not safe enough thereby,
But feard each shadow moving to and fro;
And his owne armes when glittering he did spy,
Or slashing heard, he fast away did fly,
As ashes pale of hew, and wingy heeld;
And evermore on Daunger fixt his eye,
'Gainst whom he alwaies bent a brazen shield,
Which his right hand unarmed fearefully did wield.

30. Or, as the snail, whose tender horns being hit,
Shrinks backward in his shelly cave with pain,
And there, all smother'd up, in shade doth sit,
Long after fearing to creep forth again;
So, at his bloody view, her eyes are fled
Into the deep dark cabins of her head.

31. Then hate me when thou wilt; if ever, now;
Now, while the world is bent my deeds to cross,

Join with the spite of fortune, make me bow,
And do not drop in for an after-loss :
Ah, do not, when my heart hath 'scaped this sorrow,
Come in the rearward of a conquer'd woe,
Give not a windy night a rainy morrow,
To linger out a purposed overthrow.
If though wilt leave me, do not leave me last,
When other petty griefs have done their spite,
But in the onset come; so shall I taste
At first the very worst of fortune's might,
And other strains of woe, which now seem woe,
Conpared with loss of thee will not seem so.

32. Upon the roof the bird of sorrow sat
Elonging joyful day with his sad note,
And through the shady air the fluttering bat
Did wave her leather sails and blindly float;
While with her wings the fatal screech-owl smote
Th' unblessèd house; there on a craggy stone
Celeno hung, and made his direful moan
And all about the murdered ghosts did shriek and groan.

33. Her chariot of a snail's fine shell,
Which for the colours did excel,
The fair Queen Mab becoming well
So lively was the limning;
The seat the soft wool of the bee
The cover, gallantly to see,
The wing of a pied butterfly
I trow 'twas simple trimming

34. In the first place, therefore, I thankfully acknowledge to the Almighty Power the assistance He has given me in the beginning, he prosecution, and conclusion of my present studies, which are more happily performed than I could have promised to myself, when I laboured under such discouragements. For what I have done, imperfect as it is for want of health and leisure to correct it, will be judged in after-ages, and possibly in the present, to be no dishonour to my native country, whose language and poetry would be more esteemed abroad, if they were better understood.

35. There's a bell in Moscow,
While on tower and kiosk O!
In Saint Sophia
The Turkman gets,
And loud in air
Calls men to prayer
From the tapering summits
Of tall minarets,

36. Oh how very sad I am
In my heart of hearts!
  Like bleats from a lamb
The tear from my wet eye starts.
  Down my face it runs.
Still I weep and cry,
  While suns after suns
Shine up in the bright blue sky.

37. May my dreams be granted never?
Must I aye endure affliction
Rarely realised, if ever,
In our wildest works of fiction?
Madly Romeo loved his Juliet,
Copperfield began to pine
When he hadn't been to school yet,
But their loves were cold to mine.

38. What cities, as great as this, have once triumphed in existence, had their victories as great, joy as just and as unbounded; and, with short-sighted presumption, promised themselves immortality! Posterity can hardly trace the situation of some : the sorrowful traveller wanders over the awful ruins of others; and, as he beholds, he learns wisdom, and feels the transience of every sublunary possession.

39. Passing through Tokenhouse-yard in Lothbury, of a sudden a casement violently opened just over my head and a woman gave three frightful screeches, and then cried, "O death, death, death!" in a most inimitable tone, and which struck me with horror and a chillness in my very blood. There was nobody to be seen in the whole street; neither did any other window open; for people had no curiosity now in any case; nor could anybody help one another; so I went on into Bell-alley.

40. Who has no minute's breathing space allow'd
To nurse his dwindling faculty of joy :
Joy and the outward world must die to him
As they are dead to me.
And you, ye Stars!
Who slowly begin to marshal,
As of old, in the fields of heaven,
Your distant, melancholy lines —
Have you, too, survived yourselves?
Are you, too, what I fear to become?
You, too, once lived —

41. His Wife received, the patriarch re-baptised him,
(He made the church a present, by the way),
He then threw off the garments which disguised him,
And borrowed the Count's smallclothes for a day :
His friends the more for his long absence prized him,
Finding he'd wherewithal to make them gay
With dinners, where he oft became the laugh of them,
For stories — but I don't believe the half of them.

42. O the blazing tropic night, when the wake's a welt of light That holds the hot sky tame,
And the steady fore-foot snores through the planet-powder'd floors,
Where the scared whale flukes in flame!
Her plates are scarr'd by the Sun, dear lass,
And her ropes are taut with the dew,
For we're booming down on the trail, our own trail, the out trail,
We're sagging south on the Long Trail — the trail that is always new.

43. But they thought the want of moral virtues was so far from being supplied by superior endowments of the mind, that employments could never be put into such dangerous hands as those of persons so qualified; and at least, that the mistakes committed by ignorance, in a virtuous disposition, would never be of such fatal consequence to the public weal, as the practices of a man whose inclinations led him to be corrupt, and who had great abilities to manage, to multiply, and defend, his corruptions.

44. When I look upon the tombs of the great, every emotion of envy dies in me; when I read the epitaphs of the beautiful, every inordinate desire goes out; when I meet with the grief of parents upon a tombstone, my heart melts with compassion; when I see the tombs of the parents themselves, I consider the vanity of grieving for those whom we must quickly follow; when I see kings lying by those who deposed them, when I consider rival wits placed side by side, or the holy men that divided the world with their contests and disputes, I reflect with sorrow and astonishment on the little competitions, factions, and debates of mankind. When I read the several dates of the tombs, of some that died yesterday, and some six hundred years ago, I consider that great day when we shall all of us be contemporaries, and make our appearance together.

45. I there before thee, in the country that well thou knowest,
Already arrived am inhaling the odorous air;
I watch thee enter unerringly where thou goest,
And anchor queen of the strange shipping there,
Thy sails for awnings spread, thy masts bare;
Nor is aught from the foaming reef to the snow-capped, grandest
Peak, that is over the feathery palms, more fair
Than thou, so upright, so stately, and still thou standest.

46. But while he passed before a plashy place,
A lug-worm with its gray and muddy mouth
Sang how somewhere to north or west or south
There dwelt a gay, exulting, gentle race;
And how beneath those three times blessed skies

A Danaan fruitage makes a shower of moons,
And as it falls awakens leafy tunes :
And at that singing he was no more wise.

47. No tender-hearted garden crowns,
No bosomed woods adorn
Our blunt, bow-headed, whale-backed Downs,
But gnarled and writhen thorn —
Bare slopes where chasing shadows skim,
And through the gaps revealed
Belt upon belt, the wooded, dim
Blue goodness of the Weald.

48. Him Phoebus, lending to darkness colour and form
Of light's excess, many lessons and counsels gave;
Showed Wisdom lord of the human intricate swarm,
And whence prophetic it looks on the hives that rave;
And how acquired, of the zeal of love to acquire,
And whence it stands, in the centre of life a sphere;
And Measure, mood of the lyre, the rapturous lyre,
He said was Wisdom, and struck him the notes to hear.

49. Raise me a daïs of silk and down;
Hang it with vair and purple dyes;
Carve it in doves and pomegranates,
And peacocks with a hundred eyes;
Work it in gold and silver grapes,
In leaves and silver fleurs-de-lys;
Because the birthday of my life
Is come, my love is come to me.

50. Venice seems a type
Of Life — 'twixt blue and blue extends, a stripe,
As Life, the somewhat, hangs 'twixt nought and nought :
'Tis Venice, and 'tis Life — as good you sought
To spare me the Piazza's slippery stone
Or keep me to the unchoked canals alone,
As hinder Life the evil with the good
Which make up Living, rightly understood.

51. Circle-wise sit they, with bound locks
And bosoms covered;
Into the fine cloth, white like flame,
Weaving the golden thread,
To fashion the birth-robes for them
Who are just born, being dead.

52. Here is Salome. She is a young tree
Swaying in the wind; her arms are slender branches,
And the heavy summer leafage of her hair
Stirs as if rustling in a silent wind;
Her narrow feet are rooted in the ground,
But, when the dim wind passes over her,
Rustlingly she awakens, as if life
Thrilled in her body to its finger tips.

53. We listen'd and look'd sideways up!
Fear at my heart, as at a cup,
My life-blood seem'd to sip!
The stars were dim, and thick the night,
The steersman's facc by his lamp gleam'd white;
From the sails the dew did drip.

54. Stand close around, ye Stygian set,
With Dirce in one boat convey'd!
Or Charon, seeing, may forget
That he is old and she a shade.

55. And those who husbanded the golden grain
And those who flung it to the winds like Rain
Alike to no such aureate Earth are turn'd
As, buried once, Men want dug up again.

56. As on an Alpine watch-tower
From heaven comes down the flame,
Full on the neck of Titus
The blade of Aulus came :
And out the red blood spouted,
In a wide arch and tall,
As spouts a fountain in the court
Of some rich Capuan's hall.

57. No nightingale did ever chaunt
More welcome notes to weary bands
Of travellers in some shady haunt,
Among Arabian sands :
A voice so thrilling ne'er was heard
In spring-time from the cuckoo-bird,
Breaking the silence of the seas
Among the farthest Hebrides.
Will no one tell me what she sings?—
Perhaps the plaintive numbers flow
For old, unhappy, far-off things,
And battles long ago.

58. The actors in the old tragedies, as we read, piped their iambics to a tune, speaking from under a mask, and wearing tilts and a great head-dress. 'Twas thought the dignity of the Tragic Muse required these appurtenances, and that she was not to move except to a measure and cadence. So Queen Medea slew her children to a slow music : and King Agamemnon perished in a dying fall (to use Mr. Dryden's words) : the Chorus standing by in a set attitude, and rhythmically and decorously bewailing the fates of those great crowned persons. The Muse of History hath encumbered herself with ceremony as well as her Sister of the Theatre.

59. The culprit was indeed not unworthy of that great presence. He had ruled an extensive and populous country, had made laws and treaties, had sent forth armies, had set up and pulled down princes. And in his high place he had so borne himself, that all had feared him, that most had loved him, and that hatred itself could deny him no title to glory, except virtue. He looked like a great man, and not like a bad man.

60. And Verona possesses, in the last place, the loveliest Renaissance architecture of Italy, not disturbed by pride, nor defiled by luxury, but rising in fair fulfilment of domestic service, serenity of effortless grace, and modesty of home seclusion; its richest work given to the windows that open on the narrowest streets and most silent gardens. All this she possesses, in the midst of natural scenery such as assuredly exists nowhere else in the habitable globe — a wide Alpine river foaming at her feet, from whose shore the rocks rise in a great crescent, dark with cypress, and misty with olive : illimitably, from before her southern gates, the tufted plains of Italy sweep and fade in golden light; around her, north and west, the Alps crowd in crested troops, and the winds of Benacus bear to her the coolness of their snows.

61. When she found herself abroad and in the open fields, additional subjects of apprehension crowded upon her. The dim cliffs and scattered rocks, interspersed with green sward, through which she had to pass to the place of appointment, as they glimmered before her in a clear autumn night, recalled to her memory many a deed of violence, which, according to tradition, had been done and suffered among them. In earlier days they had been the haunt of robbers and assassins, the memory of whose crimes is preserved in the various edicts which the council of the city, and even the parliament of Scotland, had passed for dispersing their bands, and ensuring safety to the lieges, so near the precincts of the city.

62. I know no handicraft, no art,
    But I have conquered fate;
For I have chosen the better part,
    And neither hope, nor fear, nor hate.
With placid breath on pain and death,
    My certain alms, alone I wait.

63. Her tears made dulcet fretting,
Her voice had no word,
More than thunder or the bird.
Yet, unforgetting,
The ravished soul her meanings knew. Mine
    ears heard not, and I heard.

64. When I stood lone on the height my sorrow did speak,
    As I went down the hill, I cried and I cried,
The soft little hands of the rain stroking my cheek,
    The kind little feet of the rain ran by my side.

65. But only a host of phantom listeners
That dwelt in the lone house then
Stood listening in the quiet of the moonlight
To that voice from the world of men :
Stood thronging the faint moonbeams on the dark stair,
That goes down to the empty hall,
Hearkening in an air stirr'd and shaken
By the lonely Traveller's call.

66. But that could not be done at once, and Tom, looking before him, saw death rushing on them. Huge fragments, clinging together in fatal fellowship, made one wide mass across the stream.

"It is coming, Maggie!" Tom said, in a deep, hoarse voice, loosing the oars, and clasping her.

The next instant the boat was no longer seen upon the water — and the huge mass was hurrying on in hideous triumph.

But soon the keel of the boat reappeared, a black speck on the golden water.

The boat reappeared — but brother and sister had gone down in an embrace never to be parted : living through again in one supreme moment the days when they had clasped their little hands in love, and roamed the daisied fields together.

67. Were it not for this voice, speaking so clearly in my conscience and my heart, I should be an atheist, or a pantheist, or a polytheist when I looked into the world. I am speaking for myself only; and I am far from denying the real force of the arguments in proof of a God, drawn from the general facts of human society (and the course of history); but these do not warm me or enlighten me; they do not take away the winter of my desolation, or make the buds unfold and the leaves grow within me, and my moral being rejoice. The sight of the world is nothing else than the prophet's scroll, full of "lamentations, and mourning, and woe."

68. Poetry is indeed something divine. It is at once the centre and circumference of knowledge; it is that which comprehends all science, and that to which all science must be referred. It is at the same time the root and blossom of all other systems of thought; it is that from which all spring, and that which adorns all, and that which, if blighted, denies the fruit and the seed, and withholds from the barren world the nourishment and the succession of the scions of the tree of life. It is the perfect and consummate surface and bloom of all things; it is as the odour and the colour of the rose to the texture of the elements which compose it, as the form and splendour of unfaded beauty to the secrets of anatomy and corruption.

69. I am the End to which the whole world strives :
    Therefore ye are girdled with a wild desire and shod
With sorrow; for among you all no soul
    Shall ever cease or sleep or reach its goal
Of union and communion with the Whole,
    Or rest content with less than being God.
Still, as unending asymptotes, your lives
    In all their myriad wandering ways
Approach Me with the progress of the golden days.

70. I go not about to inveigh against wit, for then I were witless, but frankly to confess mine own little wit. I have ever thought so superstitiously of wit, that I fear I have committed Idolatry against wisdom, and if Nature had dealt so beneficially with me to have given me any wit, I should have been readier in the defence of it to have made an Apology, than any way to turn to Apostacy.

71. But to speak in a mean. The virtue of Prosperity is temperance; the virtue of Adversity is fortitude; which in morals is the more heroical virtue. Prosperity is the blessing of the Old Testament; adversity is the blessing of the New : which carrieth the greater benediction, and the clearer revelation of God's favour. Yet even in the Old Testament, if you listen to David's harp, you shall hear as many hearse-like airs as carols; and the pencil of the Holy Ghost hath laboured more in describing the afflictions of Job than the felicities of Solomon.

72. Then, amidst the hymns and hallelujahs of saints, some one may perhaps be heard offering at high strains in new and lofty measure to sing and celebrate Thy divine mercies and marvellous judgments in this land throughout all ages; whereby this great and warlike nation, instructed and inured to the fervent and continual practice of truth and righteousness, and casting far from her the rags of her whole vices, may press on hard to that high and happy emulation to be found the soberest, wisest, and most Christian people at that day, when Thou, the eternal and shortly-expected King, shalt open the clouds to judge the several kingdoms of the world.

73. Though Somnus in Homer be sent to rouse up Agamemnon, I find no such effects in these drowsy approaches of sleep. To keep our eyes open longer were but to act our antipodes. The huntsmen are up in America, and they are already past their first sleep in Persia. But who can be drowsy at that hour which freed us from everlasting sleep? or have slumbering thoughts at that time, when sleep itself must end, and as some conjecture all shall awake again?

74. And indeed it goes so heavily with my disposition that this goodly frame, the earth, seems to me a sterile promontory; this most excellent canopy, the air, look you, this brave o'erhanging firmament, this majestical roof fretted with golden fire, why, it appears no other thing to me than a foul and pestilent congregation of vapours. What a piece of work is a man! how noble in reason! how infinite in faculty! In form and moving how express and admirable! in action how like an angel! in apprehension how like a god! the beauty of the world! the paragon of animals!

75. Darkling I listen; and for many a time
I have been half in love with easeful Death,
Call'd him soft names in many a musèd rhyme,
To take into the air my quiet breath;
Now more than ever seems it rich to die,
To cease upon the midnight with no pain,
While thou art pouring forth thy soul abroad

In such an ecstasy!
Still would'st thou sing, and I have ears in vain —
To thy high requiem become a sod.

76. Let us stay
Rather on earth, Belovèd — where the unfit
Contrarious moods of men recoil away
And isolate pure spirits, and permit
A place to stand and love in for a day
With darkness and the death-hour rounding it.

77. Sphere within sphere; and every space between
Peopled with unimaginable shapes,
Such as ghosts dream dwell in the lampless deep,
Yet each inter-transpicuous, and they whirl
Over each other with a thousand motions,
Upon a thousand sightless axles spinning,
And with the force of self-destroying swiftness,
Intensely, slowly, solemnly roll on,
Kindling with mingled sounds, and many tones,
Intelligible words and music wild.

78. The sparrow's chirrup on the roof,
The slow clock ticking, and the sound
Which to the wooing wind aloof
The poplar made, did all confound
Her sense; but most she loathed the hour
When the thick-moted sunbeam lay
Athwart the chambers, and the day
Was sloping toward his western bower.
Then, said she, "I am very dreary,
He will not come," she said;
She wept, "I am aweary, aweary,
O God, that I were dead!"

79. All that I shall now say of it is, that a good man is united unto God, as a flame touches a flame, and combines into splendour and to glory; so is the spirit of a man united unto Christ by the Spirit of God. These are the friends of God, and they best know God's mind, and they only that are so, know how much such men do know. They have a special unction from above : so that now you are come to the top of all; this is the highest round of the ladder, and the angels stand upon it : they dwell in love and contemplation, they worship and obey, but dispute not : and our quarrels and impertinent wranglings about religion are nothing else but the want of the measures of this state. Our light is like a candle; every wind of vain doctrine blows it out, or spends the wax, and makes the light tremulous; but the lights of heaven are fixed and bright, and shine for ever.

80. With these affections of mind, and my heart wholly set upon letters, I went to the university; but was soon torn from thence by that public violent storm which would suffer nothing to stand where it did, but rooted up every plant, even from the princely cedars, to me, the hyssop. Yet I had as good fortune as could have befallen me in such a tempest; for I was cast by it into the family of one of the best persons, and into the court of one of the best princesses in the world.

81. I will take heed both of a speedy friend and a slow enemy. Love is never lasting which flames before it burns; and hate, like wetted coals, throws a fiercer heat when fire gets the mastery. As quick wits have seldom sound judgments which should make them continue : so friendship kindled suddenly is rarely found to consist with the durability of affection. Enduring love is ever built on virtue, which no man can see in another at once.

82. There, as I passed with careless steps and slow,
The mingling notes came softened from below;
The swain responsive as the milk-maid sung,
The sober herd that low'd to meet their young;
The noisy geese that gabbled o'er the pool,
The playful children just let loose from school;
The watch dog's voice that bayed the whispering wind,
And the loud laugh that spoke the vacant mind.

83. They looking back all the eastern side beheld
Of Paradise, so late their happy seat,
Waved over by that flaming brand; the gate

With dreadful faces thronged and fiery arms :
Some natural tears they dropped, but wiped them soon;
The world was all before them, where to choose
Their place of rest, and Providence their guide.
They, hand in hand, with wandering steps and slow,
Through Eden took their solitary way.

84. Then lead, calm votaress, where some sheety lake
Cheers the lone heath, or some time-hallowed pile,
Or upland fallows grey
Reflect its last cool gleam.

But when chill, blustering winds, or driving rain,
Forbid my willing feet, be mine the hut,
That from the mountain's side,
Views wilds and swelling floods.

85. There hang his head, and view the lazy tide
In its hot slimy channel slowly glide;
Where the small eels that left the deeper way
For the warm shore, within the shallows play;
Where gaping mussels, left upon the mud,
Slope their slow passage to the fallen flood :
Here dull and hopeless he'd lie down and trace
How sidelong crabs had scrawled their crooked race
Or sadly listen to the tuneless cry
Of fishing gull or clanging golden-eye.

86. O eloquent, just and mighty Death! whom none could advise, thou hast persuaded; what none hath dared, thou hast done; and whom all the world hath flattered, thou only hath cast out of the world and despised : thou hast drawn together all the far-fetched greatness, all the pride, cruelty, and ambition of men, and covered it all over with these two narrow words, — *Hic jacet.*

87. If some king of the earth have so large an extent of dominion in north and south, as that he hath winter and summer together in his dominions, so large an extent east and west as that he hath day and night together in his dominions, much more hath God mercy and judgment together; He brought light out of darkness, not out of a lesser light; He can bring thy summer out of winter, though thou have no spring; though in the ways of fortune, or understanding, or conscience, thou have been benighted till now, wintered and frozen, clouded and eclipsed, damped and benumbed, smothered and stupefied till now, now God comes to thee, not as in the dawning of the day, nor as in the bud of the spring, but as the sun at noon, to illustrate all shadows, as she sheaves in harvest, to fill all penuries; all occasions invite His mercies, and all times are His seasons.

88. But the nightingale, another of my airy creatures, breathes such sweet loud music out of her little instrumental throat, that it might make mankind to think miracles are not ceased. He that at midnight, when the very labourer sleeps securely, should hear, as I have very often, the clear airs, the sweet descants, the natural rising and falling, the doubling and redoubling of her voice, might well be lifted above earth, and say, "Lord, what music hast Thou provided for the saints in heaven, when Thou affordest bad men such music on earth?"

89. Yet, by his ear directed, guessed
Something imprisoned in the chest,
And, doubtful what, with prudent care,
Resolved it should continue there.
At length a voice which well he knew,
A long and melancholy mew,
Saluting his poetic ears,
Consoled him and dispelled his fears.

90. With how sad steps, O Moon, thou climb'st the skies!
How silently, and with how wan a face!
What, may it be that even in heav'nly place
That busy archer his sharp arrows tries!
Sure, if that long-with-love-acquainted eyes
Can judge of love, thou feel'st lover's case,
I read it in thy looks; thy languisht grace,
To me, that feel the like, thy state descries.
Then, even of fellowship, O Moon, tell me,

Is constant love deem'd there but want of wit?
Are beauties there as proud as here they be?
Do they above love to be lov'd, and yet
Those lovers scorn whom that love doth possess?
Do they call virtue there ungratefulness?

91. Weep no more, woful Shepherds, weep no more,
For Lycidas your sorrow is not dead,
Sunk though he be beneath the watery floor.
So sinks the day-star in the ocean bed,
And yet anon repairs his drooping head,
And tricks his beams, and with new spangled ore
Flames in the forehead of the morning sky;
So Lycidas sunk low, but mounted high,
Thro' the dear might of Him that walked the waves.

92. Then gently scan your brother Man,
Still gentler sister Woman;
Tho' they may gang a kennin wrang,
To step aside is human :
One point must still be greatly dark,
The moving Why they do it;
And just as lamely can ye mark,
How far perhaps they rue it.

93. Bring me an axe and spade,
Bring me a winding-sheet;
When I my grave have made,
Let winds and tempests beat;
Then down I'll lie, as cold as clay,
True love doth pass away.

94. Some grounds that wept with water, or frowned with thorns, by draining the one, and clearing the other, he maketh both to laugh and sing with corn. By marl and limestones burnt, he bettereth his ground; and his industry worketh miracles, by turning stones into bread. Conquest and good husbandry both enlarge the king's dominions; the one, by the sword, making the acres more in number; the other, by the plough, making the same acres more in value.

95. In this unhappy battle was slain the Lord Viscount Falkland; a person of such prodigious parts of learning and knowledge, of that inimitable sweetness and delight in conversation, of so flowing and obliging a humanity and goodness to mankind, and of that primitive simplicity and integrity of life, that if there were no other brand upon this odious and accursed civil war, than that single loss, it must be most infamous and execrable to all posterity.

96. As in the book immediately foregoing, the Author very plainly hath pointed at the main block which lieth in the way as a hindrance to the progress of his brain-itineraries; so in this, the third of his Introduction, doth he, with great perspicacity, educe most peremptory reasons out of the clearest springs of both modern and ancient, divine and human law, why it should be removed. In the meanwhile, the better to prepare the reader towards a matter of so prime concernment, he begins the purpose with a peculiar and domestic narrative of the manner how these impediments were cast in, to the end that the more unjustly he was dealt with by the persons who did inject them, the greater justice may appear in his relief from their oppressions.

97. But most by numbers judge a poet's song;
And smooth or rough with them is right or wrong :
In the bright Muse though thousand charms conspire,
Her voice is all these tuneful fools admire;
Who haunt Parnassus but to please their ear,
Not mend their minds; as some to church repair,
Not for the doctrine, but the music there.
These equal syllables alone require,
Though oft the ear the open vowels tire;
While expletives their feeble aid do join;
And ten low words oft creep in one dull line.

98. Then comes the father of the tempest forth,
Wrapt in black glooms. First joyless rains obscure
Drive through the mingling skies with vapour foul;
Dash on the mountain's brow, and shake the woods,
That grumbling wave below. Th' unsightly plain

Lies a brown deluge; as the low-bent clouds
Pour flood on flood, yet unexhausted still
Combine, and deepening into night shut up
The day's fair face.

99. Who hath his life from rumours freed,
    Whose conscience is his strong retreat,
Whose state can neither flatterers feed,
    Nor ruin make oppressors great,

This man is freed from servile bands
    Of hope to rise or fear to fall;
Lord of himself, though not of lands,
    And having nothing, yet hath all.

100. Religion blushing veils her sacred fires,
And unawares Morality expires.
For public flame, nor private, dares to shine;
Nor human spark is left, nor glimpse divine!
Lo! thy dread empire, Chaos! is restor'd;
Light dies before thy uncreating word;
Thy hand, great Anarch! lets the curtain fall,
An universal darkness buries all.

101. At length, his transient respite past,
    His comrades, who before
Had heard his voice in every blast,
    Could catch the sound no more :
For then, by toil subdued, he drank
The stifling wave, and then he sank.

102. So pleasant their vain conceits are, that they hinder their ordinary tasks and necessary business; they cannot address themselves to them, or almost to any study or employment : these phantastical and bewitching thoughts so covertly, so feelingly, so urgently, so continually, set upon, creep in, insinuate, possess, overcome, distract, and detain them, they cannot, I say, go about their more necessary business, stave off or extricate themselves, but ever musing, melancholizing, and carried along as he (they say) that is led roundabout an heath with a *Puck* in the night.

103. For heavy lids had not long covered their lights when I thought, nay sure, I was, where I might discern all in this great *All*, the large compass of the rolling circles, the brightness and continual motion of those rubies of the night, which by their distance here below cannot be perceived; the silver-countenance of the wandering Moon, shining by another's light; the hanging of the Earth, as environed with a girdle of crystal; the Sun enthroned in the midst of the planets, eye of the heavens, and gem of this precious ring, the World.

104. Our life is short; and our days run
As fast away as does the sun :
And as a vapour, or a drop of rain
Once lost, can ne'er be found again :
So when or you or I are made
A fable, song, or fleeting shade;
All love, all liking, all delight
Lies drown'd with us in endless night.
Then while time serves, and we are but decaying,
Come, my Corinna! come, let's go a Maying.

4

Appreciation

88. Now that we have studied the elements which go to make up style, and some of the main varieties of style, we have the apparatus with which to analyse our feeling for any particular piece of prose or verse, that is, we can attempt an ordered *appreciation.*

Not, of course, that appreciation is a mere mechanical process : it is much more than that. An appreciation of any work of art is an estimation of its qualities and defects; but it is also a measure of the qualities and defects of the critic. You may easily learn to observe that a poet uses alliteration freely, that he has a simile in line 2 and a metaphor in line 4; you will not so easily decide whether his use of alliteration is beautiful or ugly, not so easily catch a glimpse of the writer's vision veiled by the simile or the metaphor.

For these, for the melody of a passage, for the colour and splendour of the words, for sublimity of thought — for the soul of the work, in short, you must train your own ear and eye and mind and soul, till in some degree they approach his. And this you can do only by reading and reading, and yet again reading — reading great books in a great way, and reading, too, the great books of Nature and Mankind from which the poet has learnt his art.

This primer does not pretend to teach you the study of nature and human nature : you must find out for yourself, if you do not already know, *how* to see the grace of a flower and the graciousness of a character. But, if you have studied the preceding chapters to any purpose, you will have already realised that reading a book is not a mere tearing from it of the story it tells or the argument it maintains, though neither story nor argument is to be despised, and the art of "skipping" is a very useful art. You will, it is hoped, have learnt to read poetry and great prose aloud, listening as you read to both time and tune, that is, rhythm and word-music; striving to see with your "inward eye," your imagination, the hues and shapes which the poet saw; trying to feel the emotions that he records, and to think his thoughts after him.

89. The first stage, then, in any appreciation is an ecstasy — a getting out of yourself into the writer; if you cannot, by stripping yourself of your own prejudices and giving yourself up completely to the author's magic, attain this ecstasy, you cannot write an appreciation. You can at best write a cool summary of the more external beauties; at worst, you will write a depreciation.

But, assuming that you have caught something of the poet's vision, the next stage is *not* the taking of a pen and the writing down of an outburst of vague praise — "This is a perfect passage, full of lovely melody and beautiful pictures," and so on. Criticisms of that sort may apply equally well to hundreds of poems; they do not help others to see the beauties you have seen; they do not even show that you *have* seen the beauties; clearly you might write exactly like this even if you had not read the passage at all. No, the next stage is a quiet turning in upon yourself, a cultivation of what Wordsworth calls "the depth and not the tumult of the soul." You must call up that mood of peaceful reminiscence which some folk experience as they day-dream curled up in front of the fire or stretched on the summer grass; but you must do this without losing the warmth of your first enthusiasm. In this mood you must go over the passage again mentally, and ask yourself first exactly *what* it is that you like. Now is the time to let your mind take charge again. Now, if you like, you may disagree with your author, find fault with him if must be. Has he aroused your delight on false pretences? Was there, even in the middle of your delight, a jarring note? If so, why did it jar? Was the fault the writer's? Has he, for instance, made one of his characters do or say something which, in the circumstances, no human being would do or say?

Or is the fault yours? Are your sympathies too narrow? Is your objection to the passage merely that it is too pious — or not pious enough — for your taste; that he is writing about cats, and you "can't bear cats"; that you had to write these lines as an imposition at school? You will be surprised to find how often it is extraneous causes such as these which interfere with your enjoyment.

90. When you have analysed your own feelings honestly and made the necessary allowances for your own prejudices, read through the passage again, trying to discover — with the help of your "apparatus" — why this phrase pleases and the other does not.

But, you may think, this is a terrible waste of time. Why not start straight away with the writing, or, at any rate, with the tabulating of beauties and defects? Well, the first reason — that such a method cannot result in a true appreciation — has already been given; the second is that what seems the longer method is really the shorter. Try; and see. The real waste of time is when you attempt to make your purely intellectual faculties do work for which they were never intended. Plunge straight into ink, and you will spend in the middle of your sentences much more time biting your pen than the preliminary "meditation" would have taken.

91. Now let us "appreciate" a passage, and see how the method works :

> Whoever comes to shroud me, do not harm
> Nor question much
> That subtle wreath of hair about mine arm;
> The mystery, the sign you must not touch,
> For 'tis my outward soul,

Viceroy to that which, unto heav'n being gone,
Will leave this to control
And keep these limbs, her provinces, from dissolution.

Let us suppose you have passed the first stage — the reading aloud with all the "expression" of which you are capable, and the soaking of yourself in the sensations so evoked — and the second — the analysis of those sensations. Compare your list with what follows :

(1) The passage needs careful reading if we are to understand it.

(2) The main idea seems far-fetched.

(3) The subject is disagreeably gruesome.

(4) We have to say "dissolution" to make the rime and rhythm right.

(5) "Subtle wreath" sounds fine; what does it mean?

(6) "Outward soul" is a striking expression.

(7) Except in the third line and very slightly in the first, there is nothing which brings a picture to our minds.

(8) There is no *marked* music in the wording; no noticeable alliteration, assonance, or onomatopoeia. On the other hand, except for the soft hissing in the last line — which is not ugly — there is no harshness, jarring, or difficulty in the sound-combinations.

(9) The last line is unintentionally funny in a grim way.

(10) The metre is light and has a pleasing lilt, the rime scheme brings into prominence the finest phrase — "outward soul."

(11) Until we reach the very last word we cannot guess what the poet is going to say; so the notion that a bracelet made of his lover's hair will keep his dead body from decaying, a notion odd enough in itself, becomes even more striking from its unexpectedness.

Some readers may have all these ideas, some only a few, some may have other ideas which do not appear in this list. The main thing is that you shall have an adequate number — say six — of *definite* conceptions, that you shall give the author a fair trial before sentencing him, and that your appreciation shall not miss all the most salient points.

Go through the list carefully then, and you will see that (4) is of no importance — clearly, when the poet wrote, the word was pronounced differently; and that (3) is of comparatively little importance — Death may be one of those subjects which we dislike, but lovers have a prescriptive right to insist that love survives death.

Of the remaining points, (2), (1), (7), (11), (8), (6), perhaps represents the order of significance; (2), at least, should be in every list.

But out of the same, materials, many different appreciations may be made; there is no absolute standard in taste. One learner may write :

> This is the very ecstasy of love. Many a lover has told us that the sight of his mistress would bring him back from the brink of the grave, but this one maintains that a bracelet of his mistress's hair will keep his dead body uncorrupted. Yet the ecstasy, though it begins with the abruptness of real passion, soon loses touch with material things, soon loses the note of sincere feeling. By the time the poet reaches his grand confession of faith — artfully reserved till the last word of the stanza — he has changed his rapture for a cold and laboured succession 'of far-fetched comparisons — the bracelet, acting as the representative of his soul, keeps his limbs from falling asunder just as a viceroy keeps the various provinces of a king's realm from severing their connection with the governing centre.
>
> The poet's inspiration, indeed, seems to have failed him a little at the end of the fifth line. After this even the rhythm is slightly uneasy — "unto heav'n being

> gone" does not run as trippingly as the rest of the passage, while all the best phrases — the finely imaginative "outward soul subtle wreath," where "wreath" suggests at once the grave and the victor, and "subtle" combines with its original sense of "thin" a hint of its later force in anticipation of "mystery"; the rare reticence of "whoever comes to shroud me" — are in the first five lines.

Another, with the last chapter fresh in his mind and convinced that valour is the better part of discretion, may say boldly :

> Clearly the writer of this passage belongs to the Metaphysical school. He has all the characteristics of Donne — his morbid preoccupation with death; his rarefied and exaggerated passion, at once divorced from sense and acutely conscious of it; his inequality — the last three lines show a distinct falling-off in poetic power; his imagination and command of the striking phrase, *e.g.* "outward soul," "subtle wreath"; his preference for the abstract — there is nothing in the stanza to call up a clear mental image, no detail, no sonorous beauty; his real command of metre, despite occasional roughness (e.g. *unto heav'n being gone,* where the slurring of *being* gives an ugly succession of sounds); his almost mystical sense of spiritual meanings behind the apparent ("the mystery, the sign you must not touch" — with a side reference to the mysteries and signs of other religions than the religion of love); his provoking fondness for far-fetched comparisons.

A third, less ambitious, will begin :

> The chief characteristic of this passage is its deliberate extravagance. The author is more concerned to be witty than to be wise; he attempts to surprise us at the expense of reason, maintaining that a hair-bracelet can preserve his body from putrefaction, *etc.* Another characteristic is the absence of concrete images, *etc.*

> Yet the author has real imagination, as we can see in his use of such phrases as "outward soul" and "subtle wreath."
>
> Nor is he without a fine sense of rhythm, *etc.*

None of these appreciations is bad; for each reflects a distinct personal opinion, and none is content merely to praise or blame blindly. A bad appreciation might run something like this :

> This writer has chosen a very gloomy subject, and has written nonsense about it. It is impossible to tell what he means; "outward soul" is rubbish — all souls are inward. One cannot call a bracelet a wreath; wreaths are worn on the head, not the arm. Nor can a wreath be subtle, since it has no mind. It is impossible, too, to question a wreath. The last three lines are quite unintelligible, and the last line has neither rime nor rhythm.

This, is a bad appreciation because it shows that the writer of it (*a*) is so conceited as to assume that what he does not understand must be nonsense; (*b*) has not sufficient intelligence and command of English to comprehend fairly difficult passage; (*c*) has not enough imagination to appreciate any kind of figure of speech; by his standards such an everyday statement as "she has fine roses in her cheeks" would be merely "nonsense"; (*d*) has not sufficient familiarity with poetry to realise that "dissolution" cannot here have its modern pronunciation.

92. Now let us examine a piece of prose :

> The provincial spirit, again, exaggerates the value of its ideas, for want of a high standard at hand by which to try them. Or rather, for want of such a standard, it gives one idea too much prominence at the expense of others; it orders its ideas amiss; it is hurried away by fancies; it likes and dislikes too passionately, too exclusively. Its admiration weeps hysterical tears, and its disapprobation foams at the mouth.... For, not

> having the lucidity of a large and centrally placed intelligence, the provincial spirit has not its graciousness; it does not persuade, it makes war, it has not urbanity, the tone of the city, of the centre, the tone which always aims at a spiritual and intellectual effect, and, not excluding the use of banter, never disjoins banter itself from politeness, from felicity.

93. The first thing which strikes us in this passage is that its *aim* is entirely different from that of the passage of poetry : it does not seek to open for us magic casements that bring fairyland before our eyes; it does not seek to raise us to an ecstasy; it seeks to convince; it appeals to our reason. This, then, gives us our method of approach : the dreamy, meditative stage of appreciation will help us little here. We shall still need to keep our senses acute, to note the sound of the passage, but we shall be merely wasting our time if we look first of all for aesthetic satisfaction. The appreciate this extract we must give the author what he asks of us — our reason.

94. Our first step, then, will be to master his argument, see whether he does, on the whole, persuade us that he is talking sense, and whether — still more important — he succeeds in making us understand what he is saying. Not, of course, that we shall give in our appreciation a summary of his ideas; such a summary is no part of a discussion of form, and would merely show that we had no clear idea of what we were attempting. But, before we can judge at all whether a writer has expressed his idea adequately, we must obviously know what idea he is trying to express.

95. The main idea of the passage is clear : the author is pointing out the defects of the "provincial spirit," the spirit which grows up in those who live isolated from the great centres of civilisation.

And, to make his point of view plain, he has recourse to that instrument with which we have already become familiar — contrast. He gives us two series of descriptions; in the first, he tells us what are the fruits of the provincial spirit; in the second, he describes the fruits of the urbane spirit. This contrast is the backbone of the passage; let us make it the backbone of our appreciation. For, just as the backbone gives the animal its shape, so this contrast gives form to the passage — it conditions the wording of almost every phrase. Let us, then, using once more our "instrument" — the knowledge of elements of style — begin our appreciation.

> This passage is a study in contrasts. First, we have the contrast which forms the root idea — the contrast between the provincial and the urbane spirit. But this contrast is not dissipated in a series of short antitheses. It is arranged in two blocks, balanced one against the other. Between these two blocks, we get ("For, not... graciousness") an explanation of the difference between the two spirits — an explanation which breaks the succession of short clauses, so avoiding monotony, and at the same time forms a perfect logical transition from one idea to the other.
>
> Much the same thing is noticeable at the beginning of the passage : the statement that "the provincial spirit exaggerates the value of its ideas" is followed, not directly by further description of the provincial spirit but, first, by an account of why there is such exaggeration, and then by a modification of the earlier description.
>
> These passages, then, are in themselves a contrast to the short, unconnected clauses which form the bulk of the passage, and which — though not strictly antitheses — have the epigrammatic value of the antithesis, since each suggests the complete contrast, one side only of which it explicitly states.
>
> The brevity of the clauses, too, helps the impression of perfect clarity which the passage gives us — a clarity attained with the use of very little concrete imagery ("weeps hysterical tears...foams at the mouth") and in spite of a large "learned" Latin element in vocabulary.

Here, as with the poetical passage, there is, of course, no standard appreciation; you are not bound to arrange your impressions in the way suggested above. You may choose the clarity of the piece as your main theme, and show in detail how the other characteristics help to give this clarity; you may show how the author maintains an attitude of sweet and persuasive reasonableness; you may show how each of the parallel clauses adds something fresh to the ideas already evoked. The only essential is that you should state in orderly fashion the impression made upon you by the passage.

Appreciation of a Character

96. That too, is the only essential of a good criticism of a character in a play on novel, or of a long work of art in prose or poetry. Suppose, for instance, you are to give your impressions of Ophelia. Just as you "meditated" upon the verse-passage for appreciation, so you will "meditate" upon Ophelia, trying to call before your mind a picture of her, trying to understand her thoughts and feelings. Then, when you feel you know her as you know your best friend, imagine yourself telling that friend what kind of girl she is. Your friend, you must suppose, has read the play for himself : but, in case he may not agree with your opinion, you will naturally refer to incidents which support your view of her character. When you have written down what you would say — assuming of course, that you and your friend are accustomed to using English, and not slang — try to discover its faults for yourself.

97. Now read the following — all appreciation intended not as a model, but as some sort of a guide —

> Ophelia is perhaps the most pathetic of Shakespeare's women. Her pompous and dogmatic father Polonius, and her fiery, self-willed brother Laertes, have trained her to be gentle, pliant, and obedient. Hence, although she loves Hamlet devotedly, she is weak enough to let herself be used as a decoy by means of which his thoughts and plans may be surprised. Hamlet's bitter

> speech of disillusion and repudiation terrifies as much as it wounds her. The death of her father and Hamlet's banishment, following closely upon this shock, shatter her intellect.
>
> Even in her madness, however, she is the same tender, graceful, creature, incapable of anger as before, and there is something symbolically appropriate in the manner of her death — floating unresistingly down-stream until she sinks.

98. You will notice that the first sentence registers the main impression produced by Ophelia, and all the rest of the appreciation amplifies and illustrates the opening statement. In that way the criticism becomes an artistic whole, not a mere series of disconnected ideas.

The second sentence gives you the root cause of her pathetic appeal — her too-yielding nature : at the same time it contrasts her with her brother and father, and suggests their share of responsibility for her fate. Next, another element in her character — her love for Hamlet — is mentioned, but the reference to it is linked naturally on to what precedes, for the chief point even here is not her love but her weakness. The following sentence gives by its allusion to her terror further evidence of that weakness, at the same time as it shows the result of her submissive complicity in her father's plot.

The final sentence of the first paragraph stresses once more her pathos; and the last paragraph gathers up all her outstanding qualities into a single picture.

You will notice that this appreciation alludes to all the main events in Ophelia's life, but that it *only* alludes to them, using them to illustrate her character : there is no attempt to give an account of her life. This is one of the chief merits of an appreciation; too often there is no clear idea in the writer's mind of whether he is writing a life or drawing a character. He may begin :

> Ophelia is a very pathetic character. She has a pompous

> old father and a bullying brother. She falls in love with Hamlet, but he is unkind to her and she goes mad. She is very gentle and sweet.

Obviously this appreciation will contain almost exactly the same information as the first, but the effect will be entirely different. In the first appreciation every sentence was another touch in the sketch of Ophelia's character; in the second, incidents in her life and traits in her character are jumbled together in the hopeless confusion — the writer has no *single purpose* in what he writes.

99. "But," you may say, "this is all very well. Everyone knows what Ophelia is like. But I may have to describe somebody in a poem or novel whose character is not so clear. What am I to do then?"

Well, if the character is not clear, the reason may be one of three — you may be dull-sighted, the author may be unskilful or the character may be exceptionally complex. It is for you to decide which reason affects the particular case. You can most easily remove your own disqualifications, as has already been hinted more than once, by a steady course of reading : reading, too, will help you to decide between the other two alternatives — though, generally speaking, it is unsafe to assume that the fault is the author's.

100. But you can also help yourself by a series of questions. — Is the character strong or weak? Kind or harsh? Good-tempered or bad-tempered? Brave or cowardly? Idle or industrious? Cheerful or sad? Commonplace or unusual? Clever or dull? How do I know which adjectives are applicable? What incidents or speeches enable me to judge? What do the other characters in the work think or say of him (or her)? How do they behave towards him (or her)? Is it probable that anybody would do, say, and think the things done, said, and thought by this character?

When you have answered all these questions and any more that occur to you, you should have a sufficiently clear idea of the character's chief traits to call up a mental picture of him in your few minutes' meditation. "But surely *after* I have analysed the character I don't need this silly meditation?" You certainly do need it — after the analysis if you cannot manage it before. Otherwise your conception of the character — and your appreciation — will lack unity, will reveal not a living character but a mere mechanical conjunction of qualities.

Appreciation of a Novel

101. Much the same method may be adopted if you have to appreciate a novel. Let us take *David Copperfield* as an example and think ourselves back to the time when we first read it. Let us call up the glow of satisfied excitement with which we closed the book and try to discover what caused that glow. Here, perhaps, the very lapse of time will help us. What stands out most clearly in our memory now, we can be very sure is what made the deepest impression upon us then. What pictures, then, do we see when we shut our eyes and use the words "David Copperfield" as our "Open Sesame." First, probably, David as a youngster at home, then David with the Peggotty family, then David at Mr. Creakle's, and so on. But as the pictures succeed one another, we find that David himself figures in them less frequently. This, then, will give us a "main idea" round which to group our impressions. For the rest here, as in our account of Ophelia, we must be careful not to be led astray from our theme by a desire to enlarge upon some subsidiary episode — Little Em'ly's story, say, or the death of Dora. A passing reference, some single adjective or noun which gives our feeling on the subject, is all that we can allow ourselves. Perhaps the final result will be something like this :

> *David Copperfield*, often reckoned Dickens's greatest book, owes much of its fame to the psychological truth with which David's childish feelings are portrayed. The interest with which we follow his friendship with the Peggotty family, his brief experience of Mr. Creakle, the hardships of his life in the warehouse after his mother's death, his school days, and his boyish love

> for Dora Spenlow, changes imperceptibly as the story advances from an interest in David to an interest in the plot and in the other characters, but this is due as much to the attractions of the inimitable Micawber, the scoundrelism of Uriah Heep, and the pathos of Little Em'ly's history as to any loss of reality in David himself. He retains our sympathies even in his second marriage, though Agnes has not Dora's charm.

Or we may find ourselves in disagreement with the orthodox view and write :

> *David Copperfield is* generally praised as primarily a wonderful picture of child life. It is true that young David is a very vivid little figure — though no more vivid perhaps than young Pip in *Great Expectations.* But the main interest of the story surely does not lie there : if it did, the greater part of the book would have to be reckoned a failure. No : for most of us *David Copperfield* means Micawber and his absurd optimism and the moving if melo-dramatic tale of Little Em'ly. Beside these bright realities the empty-headed Dora and the stockishly pious Agnes are but dim fancies from the realm of Never-Was.

Nor, of course, do these two appreciations at all exhaust the ways in which the novel may be criticised. You may take as your main theme Dickens's love of dramatic situations, the gallery of caricatures which he gives us, his ability to tell an interesting tale, his fondness for springing surprises on the reader, or any one of half-a-dozen more.

Appreciation of a Play

102. An appreciation of a play hardly differs from an appreciation of a novel, unless you are criticising the acting as well as the play itself. Here, as with the novel, you must not attempt to give the plot; here, as with the novel, you must — if you are to avoid a meaningless cloud of phrases — refer freely to incidents and characters in the play; here, as with the novel, your impressions should be threaded on some connecting idea, not mere loose beads scattered haphazard.

103. Take an account of *King Lear*, for instance :

> *King Lear* is in the intensity of its passion the greatest of Shakespeare's tragedies. Its theme is filial ingratitude, and it follows the general rule of Shakespeare's tragedies in that disaster is brought about by some weakness in the central characters, Lear in the main plot and Gloucester in the under-plot. But here, more even than in *Hamlet,* "the time is out of joint" and Lear's tremendous denunciations are not too fierce for the monstrous crimes by which he is surrounded. For it is not only the treatment meted out to him by his daughters Goneril and Regan and to Gloucester by the latter's son Edmund that produces the tragic gloom of the play. Lear himself passes from the consideration of his personal wrongs to curses on the general foulness of "this great stage of fools." The tempest, the wild heath, the madness, all increase the impression of something unbalanced in the very constitution of the universe; and the Fool, who acts as chorus till there is no longer place for even his poor cheerfulness, has in fact no brighter comment on life to offer than has Lear himself.

Here the main theme — the passionate intensity of the play — is given in the first sentence, and the whole of what follows amplifies and illustrates that preliminary statement. From the more obvious points — the tragic events of the plot, and Lear's denunciations — we pass to those subtler matters of background and tragic-comic relief which give "atmosphere," and divide the great tragedian from the skilful constructor of rhetorical melodrama. And, as in the case of the novel, there is no reason why we should not write a score of other appreciations, each dealing with some particular aspect : the only difference, perhaps, is that with the play we may find it convenient to criticise the development of the subject act by act, whereas the greater length and complexity of the novel make an ordered survey from beginning to end impossible.

Appreciation of a Poem

104. At first sight the appreciation of a poem is a more difficult matter. In reality, however, involves little that is new to us. We have already seen bow to deal intensively with a short passage of verse; we have already seen how to criticise a long work of art : if we combine the two we shall know how to appreciate a poem. We must consider the style : is it ornate or simple, imaginative or pedestrian, pictorial, musical, full of thought, marked by contrasts, full of epigrams? We must consider the aim of the poet : does he achieve it? In the case of a long poem we must consider the structure : is the story well told, the argument skilfully developed, the arrangement of the parts good? Briefly, the criticism of a short poem approximates to that of a passage of verse, while the criticism of a long poem approximates to that of a novel or play.

If we take Wordsworth's *Alice Fell* we shall need the qualities of both types, for, although the poem is short, it is not a "swallow flight of song" : it is a story whose value depends at least as much on the theme and narrative as on the beauty of the wording. Our appreciation, then, may run something like this :

> Wordsworth's theories as to the nature of poetry often had an unhappy effect upon his art, and he achieved some of his best work by ignoring those theories. In *Alice Fell,* however, he succeeds in producing a poem which both satisfies the lover of poetry and conforms to his own canons. Its subject — the grief of an orphan child whose tattered cloak is caught in the wheels of a postchaise — could not well be more simple; the diction and metre are as simple as the subject. Yet, through the force of his sympathetic imagination, the poet produces with these slight materials a genuinely pathetic effect. To Alice Fell her ragged cloak is as much as is his kingdom to a monarch : tragedy,

> Wordsworth shows us, is constituted by the quality and depth of emotion, not by the importance of the material cause which evokes it.

Here the emphasis is divided fairly equally between style and matter, the connecting link being the simplicity apparent in both. If we had been considering Goldsmith's *Deserted Village*, however, we should have been obliged to give less space in proportion to comments upon the way in which the poem is written, and more to an appreciation of what it is written about — the village and the people in it. If, on the other hand, we had been criticising a short lyric like Herrick's "Fair Daffodils, we weep," our appreciation would have been to all intents and purposes an "appreciation of a verse passage."

Appreciation of a Non-fiction Prose Work

105. The same is true of any non-fiction prose work. An appreciation of Lamb's *Dream Children* might read :

> *Dream Children* is perhaps the greatest of Lamb's Essays, combining his whimsicality and fanciful imagination with the peculiar wistful pathos of which he is, at will, a master. The slight strokes of description, the little touches which give the very manner and nature of children — "Here John smiled, as much as to say, 'that would be foolish indeed' " ... "Here Alice's little right foot played an involuntary movement till, upon my looking grave, it desisted" — make of these, who "are nothing, less than nothing, and dreams," two of the most real and gracious child figures in literature.

This criticism contains a good deal of detail; but if our appreciation were of Lamb's *Essays* as a whole we should be obliged to take a more general view — to quote less, to say more of Lamb's characteristics, something of his choice of subject, a little perhaps of the influences which helped to make his prose what it was. But, whatever we say, the same guiding axioms are applicable — a good sentence at the beginning, a better sentence at the end, and in between a stout, straight connecting thread.

You will, indeed, probably have realised by this time that, however important it may be in an appreciation to say the right thing, it is vastly more important to say something — anything — in the right way.

EXERCISE IV

1. Write an appreciation of each of the passage in Exercise III.

2. Write an appreciation of (*a*) your favourite novel, (*b*) your favourite short story, (*c*) your favourite poem.

3. Write appreciations of *As You Like It*, *School for Scandal*, *Hamlet*, Galsworthy's *Justice*, Flecker's *Hassan*, *The Rivals*, *Twelfth Night*, *She Stoops to Conquer*, *The Beggar's Opera*, Barrie's *The Will*, Shaw's *Candida*, *The Mikado*.

4. Which of the two appreciations of *David Copperfield* given in the last chapter do you prefer? Why?

5. Write appreciations of Sam Weller, Mrs. Proudie, Mr. Collins (in *Pride and Prejudice*), Mrs. Gamp, Andrew Fairservice, Jeanie Deans, Mrs. Dombey, Mr. Micawber, Diana of the Crossways, Mrs. 'Arris (in *Martin Chuzzlewit*), the Fool in *Lear*, Charles Surface, Becky Sharp, Maggie Tulliver, Miranda, Tess D'Urberville, Mr. Lewisham (in *Love and Mr. Lewisham*).

6. Write a critical account of each of the following : *Lamia Adonais, Lycidas, Rob Roy, The De Coverley Papers, Treasure Island, Childe Harold, The Ancient Mariner, The Passing of Arthur,* Shelley's *Ode to a Skylark,* Macaulay's *Essay on Clive, Comus, Adam Bede, Jane Eyre, Kenilworth,* Wells's *Kipps,* Masefield's *Dauber,* Kipling's *First Jungle Book.*

7. Which of the passages in Exercise III remind you of (*a*) Keats, (*b*) Spenser; and why?

Index

The main reference is in each case given first.

The numbers refer in general to pages. Sometimes, however, a number is followed by a second number in parentheses, *e.g.* 86 (60). This signifies that the reference is to an *exercise*, page 86, passage 60.

The reader is thus enabled to look up with the aid of the index all comments on the author he is studying, and then, when he has completed his work, to turn to exercises on that author.

The passages in Exercise III are indexed last under their respective authors; hence any curious reader can discover the writers with comparatively little trouble.

In the case of the best-known writers it has been considered unnecessary to add remarks.

C

D

E

F

G

H

I

J

K

T